THE ST

THE STALKER AFFAIR

Frank Doherty

THE MERCIER PRESS
Cork and Dublin

The Mercier Press, 4 Bridge Street, Cork.
24 Lower Abbey Street, Dublin 1

BRITISH LIBRARY CATALOGUING IN PUBLICATION DATA

Doherty, Frank
The Stalker Affair.
1. Ireland. *Garda Síochána* 2. Secret
service — Great Britain — History — 20th century.
1. Title
363.2'09417 HV8198.A2

ISBN 0-85342-795-X

Typesetting by Alphaset, Limerick.

Printed by Litho Press Co., Midleton, Co. Cork.

Contents

Introduction

This is a book about an alleged cover-up. Mention the name John Stalker and many people will be aware that the subject in question is Deputy Chief Constable John Stalker, second in command of the Greater Manchester Constabulary.

Stalker was asked in May, 1984, to investigate the circumstances relating to a number of deaths in Co. Armagh which had resulted from a series of shootings by RUC officers. His brief, following the acquittal of an RUC man on charges relating to the deaths of two INLA men, Seamus Grew and Roddy Carroll, was to examine three specific incidents to determine if claims made by Catholic clergymen and Nationalist politicians that the RUC was operating a shoot-to-kill policy of summary execution of suspected gunmen were true, and to make whatever recommendations were necessary as a result.

What Stalker and the eight Manchester CID detectives he brought with him to Northern Ireland found may have shocked him. Investigating the Armagh killings was like pulling on a ball of string. The more it was teased out, the more there seemed left to unravel. His enquiries took him beyond the simple facts about the shootings. Interference with forensic evidence, perjury, clandestine missions across the border into the Irish Republic — all these had been discovered and recorded when Stalker and his team moved on to the most sensitive part of his investigation.

He wanted to know who was behind this web of criminal intrigue — and why. But by now he was well beyond where those in authority expected he would go. After two years he was still beavering away, refusing to accept evasions or excuses from any quarter. After all, although nominally appointed by Sir John

Hermon, the Chief Constable of the RUC, the decision to send Stalker to Belfast had been made by the Home Office Inspectorate of Constabulary on the orders of the Home Secretary — and this meant that Mrs Margaret Thatcher herself had approved.

John Stalker had the authority to probe into the secret nooks and crannies of the security system in Northern Ireland, and as a criminal investigation detective of twenty-five years standing he had the experience to do it. But he reckoned without the secret and sinister forces which are part of the political and military mix in Northern Ireland.

Two years almost to the day after his appointment, with his investigations leading higher and higher in London, John Stalker found himself disgraced as a policeman and out of the inquiry, first on enforced leave, then under suspension. The hunter had become the hunted. Stalker the investigator was himself the investigated, and a campaign of smears and innuendo ensured that no matter what might happen from then on, John Stalker, the honest cop, would always be known as John Stalker, the controversial cop, the man who had been under a cloud about his personal behaviour and his integrity as a police officer.

The Stalker affair is something that goes well beyond the question of guilt or innocence in the killings of a handful of young Irishmen. It goes higher than the senior officers who commanded the men with the guns, farther than the missions into the Irish Republic which were admitted under oath in Belfast Crown Court. Stalker is to British intelligence and its political masters what Watergate was to the Americans and the *Rainbow Warrior* was to the French.

Unlike Watergate, which showed the American mass media at its crusading best, and the *Rainbow Warrior* affair, where the multi-facet nature of the French press ensured that leak after leak was published in newspapers of the right or left until the full story emerged, the British mass media has no history of exposing high level scandals involving the intelligence and political establishment. Down the years, the British public have been treated to a series of spy revelations, but invariably they have involved individuals, or small groups of traitors, whose most intimate secrets were connected with their sex lives.

Those who expect Fleet Street or the BBC to tell the full story of the Stalker affair should think again. The British media is too well controlled by the establishment in London to allow a scandal of Watergate dimensions to be revealed. Even Prime Minister Harold Wilson found this to be the case, too late, and to his cost. Wilson's claim that M15 ran a smear campaign against him in an effort to destabilise his leadership (which proved to be successful) has never been probed in the establishment media in Britain. The network of interlocking club memberships, old school links, the honours system, the centralisation of the upper levels of British society in a small area of London over which the royal family preside, all ensure that scandals are contained within proper boundaries. Individuals may be disgraced and hounded, but no whiff of impropriety will be allowed to affect the structures of the establishment, even years after the event.

The sacrificing of Stephen Ward, the pimping osteopath in the John Profumo scandal of the 1960s, has just recently been revealed. But the reason behind it has not. While John Profumo was pilloried in the British media for dallying with a woman he allegedly shared with an alleged KGB agent, the role of M15 in the affair and in covering up what really went on has never been exposed. There have been other examples of the British media quietly losing interest in intriguing reports of intelligence double-dealing.

The wider aspects of the Anthony Blunt case — who covered up, and why, have been ignored while irrelevant aspects of his private life have been paraded in a confusing collection. More recent possible intelligence scandals have been left untouched. The links between the Kincora Boys' Home sex scandal and Sir Maurice Oldfield have gone largely unrecorded in the British press, not out of deference to the memory of the deceased spy chief, but because of the risks of exposing the shadier side of the cover-up. Many people connected with Kincora have died in sudden and mysterious circumstances. Were these drownings, suicides and deaths at the hands of gunmen all coincidence? Fleet Street was preparing to expose Oldfield's unusual fondness for young males, but someone, somewhere, intervened and the story has never been published in a British newspaper, despite the great amount of time and money spent by reporters who camped out on the doorstep of his London flat for weeks waiting for the move that would allow them to jump the legal hurdles in mentioning him.

There have been many other examples of scandals which might affect the British intelligence structures, as distinct from individuals, being ignored. Allegations made by Captain Fred Holroyd formerly of the Special Military Intelligence Unit (Northern Ireland) about criminal offences being carried out on both sides of the Irish border, including alleged kidnaps, murders and the planting of explosives, have been largely ignored. So have similar claims made by several independent sources about intelligence operations in Ireland, including those made by an officer who spent seven years at the centre of such activity in the British Military Intelligence Irish headquarters in Lisburn, Captain Colin Wallace. A week after Stalker's suspension, a former senior M15 officer now living in retirement in Australia, Peter Wright, was effectively gagged from talking about some of the dirty tricks he had seen in the organisation. The British Attorney-General obtained an injunction against him publishing such details, saying he was bound to silence under the Official Secrets Act. There seems to be no reason to believe that the Stalker affair with its likelihood of uncovering the seamier side of British intelligence operations will fare any differently.

It is perhaps one of the great wonders of the modern world that the British intelligence services manage to keep themselves so well distanced from publicity, given the vast numbers of personnel involved and the amount of money spent. After the Soviet Union and the United States, Britain has the world's largest espionage, counter-intelligence and eavesdropping services. A strike in one espionage group in 1984 — the Signals Intelligence listening system known as GCHQ — revealed that it had 10,000 employees in Britain. A similar number are stationed in other parts of the world. The amount spent by Britain on all forms of intelligence may be as much as 10% of total defence expenditure, according to *The Financial Times,* a figure which puts the funds available each year for this secretive and often sinister work at more than £12,000 million, from the British exchequer alone. Additional funds come from the Americans for agency services overseas and at GCHQ.

Those journalists in Britain who have tried to probe deeper into intelligence matters, beyond the titillating minor sex scandals which surface with monotonous regularity, have run into trouble. Duncan Campbell, now a writer with the *New Statesman* magazine, and his freelance colleague Crispin Aubrey were prosecuted under the Official Secrets Act in 1977, along with a former army NCO contact, for collecting details on Britain's vast eavesdropping system.

Campbell got into trouble again when he was in contact with Captain Fred Holroyd, the ex-intelligence man making allegations about dirty tricks in Ireland. In February, 1984, he was knocked off his bicycle by a car in London and taken to hospital with head injuries. Documents in panniers on the bike were seized under the Official Secrets Act and his home was raided under the same Act while he was still in hospital, with more papers being taken. Other journalists were threatened with prosecution and jail if they dared publish the information on British espionage they had obtained in respect of Central America. They did not publish it.

American journalist Mark Hosenball, who worked with ex-CIA officer Phillip Agee to up-date information on British eavesdropping, was deported for his efforts, as was Agee. Jonathan Bloch, a refugee journalist from South Africa was told he had to leave Britain having written about Her Majesty's intelligence services. Other media investigators have been given a carrot instead of a stick in an effort to persuade them to move in the direction which suited British intelligence. A number of journalists in Britain changed their views on how far organisations like M15 and M16 should be exposed when they obtained lucrative jobs with establishment publications.

It is against this background that the Stalker drama is set. The British media have reported the affair extensively, but not in depth. There have been tales about freemason influence and clashes between RUC Chief Sir John Hermon and the Manchester investigator — as though these were the most important aspects of what happened. Other red herrings have included reports about a mysterious bugged M15 tape recording said to have been made at the scene of one shooting. Investigation shows that M15 do not carry out routine surveillance in Northern Ireland — leaving such matters to their operational arm, the RUC's E4A unit, indicating that this may have been introduced as a distraction from other issues in the case.

Stalker, the veteran policeman and ace detective who had his share of brushes with some of Britain's most dangerous criminals, was a frightened man. He told his wife he believed his life was in danger because of what he had discovered in Northern Ireland.

Just as an apparently simple break-in at the Watergate office building in Washington led to massive revelations about American intelligence operations and a series of scandals about the conduct of the war in Vietnam, Stalker's insistence on continuing to pull at the Irish ball of string threatened to unravel secrets that went way beyond his anticipated brief. While Watergate proved a disaster for the CIA and ultimately the administration of President Nixon, the Stalker inquiry threatened to lay bare information which would have the same effect on British intelligence and key figures in London.

There was only one thing to be done. Stalker had to be stopped, one way or another. He was.

Whatever the outcome of the investigation he commenced in 1984, however the final report is drafted, attention has already been distracted from it. The Stalker affair now is about the suspension of a Manchester policeman, and the rights and wrongs of that action — not about the shoot-to-kill incidents, the illegal operations of British intelligence, or the political figures who authorised them.

1. The Shooting of Carroll and Grew

At 8.20 pm on the night of 12 December 1982, Joe Graham was walking along the road to Killylea, outside Armagh. It was sharply cold with good visibility. An old Austin Allegro approached, its engine straining as it ascended the hill. Graham glanced at the driver. It was an instinctive reaction. In that part of the world, at that time of day, it was a sensible precaution. Many Catholic men had been shot in Armagh by travelling gunmen firing from passing cars. Despite its claim to city status, Armagh is a small town, where almost everybody knows everyone else.

As the car slowed to take a bend, he waved a greeting to its driver — a man well-known to him, Seamus Grew. Although Graham could not see clearly the features of the person in the passenger seat he was to discover his identity soon, in a dramatic fashion: for Grew and his companion, Roddy Carroll were just seconds away from death. A few hundred feet further along the road to Carroll's home in Mullacreevie Park they would die in a hail of bullets, and in an incident that was to prove as significant for British intelligence as the break-in at the Watergate building in Washington in June, 1972, was for the American Central Intelligence Agency.

At exactly 8.25 pm Fr Patrick McDonnell received a telephone call from a distraught parishioner. There had been a shooting. Two men were hurt, a priest was needed. Within minutes, Fr McDonnell, was on the scene. A uniformed RUC man, one of a number grouped around the car parked neatly at the side of the road, told him that Seamus Grew had been shot.

The priest knew Grew and his family. There were few Catholic families in Armagh Fr McDonnell, the administrator of St Patrick's Parish (of which the Archbishop of Armagh, Cardinal Tomás Ó Fiaich, was the titular head) did not know, as parishioners and friends. He knew the man in the passenger seat — Roddy Carroll, a 22-year-old member of one of the most politically active families in the town. Neither Grew nor Carroll were wanted for questioning about any crime. Neither were armed.

The priest began the ritual of prayer for the dying. The RUC man in charge ordered him away from the scene, but not before Fr McDonnell, a man well used to sudden and violent death after years of bloody trouble in Armagh, counted thirteen bullet holes in the passenger door of the vehicle and two bullet holes in the rear on the driver's side. The back window of the car had been shattered.

He noted that Roddy Carroll was slumped, face down, his body turned across the driver's seat as though trying to escape from a hail of gunfire which had come through the passenger door. The priest ignored RUC orders and walked to the other side of the vehicle. He found Seamus Grew lying face up on the road in a pool of blood.

No one seemed to know what had happened. Neighbours who stood around in stunned silence believed both men were victims of sectarian murderers from a Loyalist paramilitary group. One woman who dashed from her home in Mullacreevie Park having heard gunfire saw three men standing near the car wearing dark Bridgedale, military-style sweaters with arm and shoulder patches, dark trousers and waist-belts with holsters. None had headgear. None looked like policemen.

The man who fired the fatal shots had left the scene. He was an Englishman and ex-soldier, RUC Constable John Robinson, a 29-year-old member of a secret squad set up for counter-terror operations, the Special Support Unit of 'E' Department, RUC Headquarters. It was 10 o'clock that night before the people of Armagh learned that the deaths of Grew and Carroll had been caused by a security forces' shooting. It was four hours before a statement claiming Grew and Carroll failed to stop at a roadblock was issued by the RUC. The following day, Fr Raymond Murray, another Armagh priest, began to piece together details of what happened. He and his friend, Fr Denis Faul, had for years been systematically recording abuses of power by the authorities in

Northern Ireland. Fr Murray had dossiers on more than 100 deaths which he described as being those of people 'completely innocent ... deliberately shot dead in cold blood by the British Army, RUC or UDR.' Now he had another two names on his files.

Bit by bit, the two investigating priests began to fit together the jig-saw of events on the night of the fatal shootings. Eye-witnesses, too terrified to be named, told how they had seen Grew's car being driven at normal speed along the Keady road into Armagh. A dark Peugeot, travelling at high speed had overtaken it near Mullacreevie Park, forcing it to stop. A burst of gunfire was heard, followed by two single shots.

Within twenty-four hours of the killings, enough evidence had become available for local dignitaries to express concern about what had happened. Predictably, the leading Nationalist politician in the area, Seamus Mallon, deputy leader of the Social Democratic and Labour Party, demanded some answers from the Northern Ireland Secretary of State, Jim Prior, and the RUC Chief Constable, Jack Hermon. The Grew-Carroll killings had been the latest in a series of mysterious fatal shootings by even more mysterious RUC men. Mallon challenged the two security bosses to state publicly that an SAS-style squad, authorised to kill people on suspicion, was not operating in the RUC. In the absence of such a statement he could only assume that there was such a policy, and that the 'law of the jungle' was being applied.

Mallon was not the only one to publicly voice his concern at what had happened. Cardinal Ó Fiaich, having consulted the priest who tried to give the men the last rites of the Catholic Church, as well as Denis Faul and Raymond Murray, decided to make his views known. Coincidentally, he and his Protestant counterpart as Primate of Ireland and Archbishop of Armagh, Dr John Armstrong, were to make their annual pastoral visit to the Northern Ireland Office at Stormont Castle. They arrived together in James Prior's office for what was to have been a routine exchange of views on the state of affairs in the area during the past year and the likely course of events in the coming year of 1983.

It was Archbishop Armstrong who raised the Grew-Carroll killings. He told Prior that he was concerned about police tactics, that there were many people who were upset at some of the recent deaths, like those of the two Armagh men the previous night. His remarks, published in the media within hours of the meeting, were greeted with annoyance by senior Unionist politicians who, while not prepared to openly take a line opposing the Protestant church leader's view, were of the opinion that Catholics, especially politically active Catholics suspected of being linked with Republican groups, were fair game for the guns of the RUC.

Cardinal Ó Fiaich made a protest to Prior about the Armagh deaths. He knew from long experience that quiet words said behind closed doors about such matters had little effect on the British authorities. When he returned to his home at Ara Coeli, a short distance from where the fatal shootings happened, he had further consultations with local priests. The blatant nature of the killings, the obvious embarrassment of the security authorities over the incident and the unexplained four-hour delay by the RUC in admitting that they were involved all added up to a disturbing situation. The Cardinal, with the full authority vested in his office by the Catholic Church, issued a statement that was not going to be easily ignored.

The deaths of the two men on Sunday night, according to Cardinal Ó Fiaich's statement, coming so soon after the deaths in similar circumstances in the Lurgan area of Co. Armagh over the past month or so, was a cause of great disquiet. He said until the full details of these deaths were known many important questions remained unanswered.

It was a subdued and carefully worded pronouncement, containing little hint of the burning anger in the Nationalist community throughout Northern Ireland at these latest deaths in what SDLP politicians had dubbed the RUC's shoot-to-kill policy.

Reaction in the community was different. Archbishop Armstrong's concern at RUC tactics reflected only a minority view, that of the increasingly rare, Unionist middle class people who were upset at what could be seen as a further twist of the screw of violence, with the RUC apparently turning to roadside summary executions — a situation which they knew could only make things more vicious and increase the risk to themselves and their families.

Other Loyalists were less circumspect in their reaction. Most were delighted at what they saw as another example of the RUC's gloves-off policy with Nationalists. Not for the first time, the opinion could be heard in Unionist heartlands that the only good Fenian was a dead Fenian — especially if he was, as Grew and Carroll were, a member of the Irish National Liberation Army, the smaller and more ruthless offshoot of the IRA.

The fact that Seamus Grew, a 31-year-old married man with a nine-year-old son, and Roderick Martin Carroll, a 22-year-old unmarried man, both natives of Armagh, were claimed by the INLA as members of that organisation within hours of the shooting surprised no one in the town. Their links with the Irish Republican Socialist Party, the political wing of the INLA were quite open. But both lived openly at home, and neither was wanted for any crime. Less than a month earlier, they had been in the hands of the Ulster Defence Regiment having been stopped at a road-check, but were allowed to proceed after the intervention of a local priest.

A statement issued by six priests in the parish of Armagh hours after their death gave details of this incident. It read:

> Following a message at mid-day on November 19th to the parochial house that Seamus Grew and Roderick Carroll were being threatened with death at a UDR checkpoint, a priest from the parish went to the scene, verified the threat and, seeing their distraught state, stayed for about 20 minutes until he was ordered to leave by the UDR officer in charge. The priest concerned assured the two men that they were safe because he had tape-recorded his interview with the UDR officer at the scene.

On the night they died, Seamus Grew and Roddy Carroll were returning from Monaghan in Grew's car, having left Carroll's sister, Irene, at her home there. Earlier, they had attended the funeral in Magherafelt, Co. Derry, of the Carroll's maternal grandfather. They left Monaghan after 7 pm and drove west towards Keady, taking the back road into Armagh which was regularly used by Nationalists to avoid hold-ups or harassment at the permanent British army fortified border crossing at Middleton on the main road. Did they meet someone in Keady or along their 12-mile route to death, or were they halted at one of the many random UDR, British Army or RUC road-checks often set up along that road? That will probably never be known.

In the event, it took nearly an hour longer than should have been necessary for them to reach that fateful spot outside Armagh where they met their death. The theory must remain that they spoke to another well-known Republican, one who, unlike them, was urgently being sought by the RUC, alive or dead ... a man they had met and spoken to the night before in the home of an informer in Castleblaney. That man was Dominic McGlinchey.

An RUC statement issued in the aftermath of the Grew and Carroll killings said Grew had driven his car through a police road-check, hitting and injuring a policeman, and that RUC men at the check-point had fired on the fleeing vehicle. They later admitted that this was a false version of events.

The Armagh County Coroner, Gerard Curran, made repeated requests for information which would allow him to open an inquest. He was told this would not be available until the RUC had completed their investigations and the Director of Public Prosecutions had decided if a criminal prosecution should be started. Newspaper queries to the DPP's office six months after the killings brought the response that the question of whether or not an inquest is to be held or adjourned 'is a matter for H.M. Coroner.' Nine months after the shootings neither the RUC nor the DPP had taken any action, nor had they given the coroner any reason for the delay.

On 3 September 1983, Gerard Curran brought the issue into the open. Speaking at a routine inquest hearing, he said:

> Apart from the autopsy reports which I received from the pathologist in March, not a single statement or document has been made available to me (about the Grew and Carroll deaths). I have a public duty to hold every inquest as soon as practicable, and this duty has been largely negated by the unexplained delay by the DPP. Such unexplained delay has caused the agony of suspense and a sense of frustration to all concerned which is contrary to the principles of natural and constitutional justice.

The coroner's action provoked a swift reaction from the DPP, Barry Shaw. Within a matter of weeks the ex-soldier turned RUC special operations constable, John Robinson, had been charged with murdering Seamus Grew. No charge was laid in respect of Roddy Carroll. Like other security forces members accused of serious crimes, Constable Robinson was remanded into the custody of his superiors.

Robinson went on trial on 20 March 1984 in a Diplock Court held in the Belfast Crown Court Building at Crumlin Road. Diplock Courts represent a system of justice unique to Northern Ireland. They take their name from Lord Diplock, the British law expert who recommended that juries be eliminated from criminal trials which involved cases of a political nature or violence which had political links. A lone judge hears the evidence, sums it up, and then directs himself to bring in a verdict of guilty or not guilty.

On 3 April 1984, Robinson was acquitted of the charge of murdering Seamus Grew, by Mr Justice MacDermott. There are no transcripts of the trial available. These are only issued to an accused's legal advisors in the event of an appeal. However, to quote Mr Justice MacDermott's summing up:

> ...While policemen are required to work within the law, they are not required to be supermen...I am satisfied that the accused honestly believed he had been fired at and that his life was in danger.

Referring to claims made by Constable Robinson in the witness box that he had been ordered by senior RUC officers to lie in court about the shooting to cover aspects of the operation, including the fact that the RUC Special Branch was carrying out a mission in the Irish Republic, Justice MacDermott said: 'I am not in this case conducting an inquiry into why the officers who advised, instructed or constrained the accused acted as they did...My task throughout has been to decide whether or not the accused is guilty as charged.' There was evidence that Robinson had been given 'advice and instructions' and had constraints placed upon him by the Official Secrets Act, yet it was difficult to see how this helped Robinson's case.

Addressing himself in the absence of a jury, Justice MacDermott went on:

> This claim was not disputed by the Crown...Neither the police as such, nor those officers in particular are represented in these proceedings or charged with anything... the true facts should be ascertained, if that be possible, as quickly as possible and that a person who may have to face a charge of murder (or indeed any charge) should not be required to tell a false story...if his statement contained secret or operationally important matters then arrangements for editing, if appropriate, could have been made.

Although Robinson's version of events was 'distorted' said the judge this could be explained because events were happening faster than the time it takes to describe them and the accused was not telling lies and had not sought to tally his story with the forensic evidence. There were forensic matters which were speculative rather than conclusive (this allowed him to ignore a startling claim made by the Crown prosecutor, instructed by the DPP, obviously anxious to stay clear of any cover-up, that forensic evidence had been interfered with). Mr Justice MacDermott said he was not required to give an explanation for his 'not guilty' verdict, but he had decided to do so because of the circumstances of the case.

He said Constable Robinson was a member of an RUC mobile support unit specially trained to fight terrorism, who had been sent from Belfast to Armagh.

> ...The members of the unit had been sent to Armagh as the police authorities believed, as a result of information from their intelligence sources, that a man called McGlinchey was coming over the border from the Republic of Ireland....McGlinchey was a man believed to be deeply involved in terrorist activities on both sides of the border, a dangerous and determined man....The deceased Grew was also known to be a member of the INLA.

Neither of these men would have had any qualms about resisting arrest, said the judge. He then told Robinson he was free to go.

That might have been the end of the matter. But Robinson, seemingly determined that he was not going to become a scapegoat for an officially authorised mission which had gone wrong and attracted a lot of adverse publicity, had already said too much in court.

In response to questions from his defence counsel he said he was part of a special team sent to trap INLA leader Dominic McGlinchey. The prosecution alleged that he had shot Carroll at close range, emptying his pistol, before reloading it and walking to the other side of the car, where he shot the driver, Seamus Grew. Confronted with this, Constable Robinson claimed some of his statements had been untrue. He had been ordered to tell lies to cover up the nature of his mission. He wrote down the names of three senior officers who had given him those instructions and handed the piece of paper to Mr Justice MacDermott. Robinson had had his day in court, admitted he had shot both Carroll and Grew many times from a distance of a few feet, and walked free. But that was not to be the end of the matter. The trial of Constable John Robinson had lifted the lid on what *The Irish Press* was to later describe as 'a can of worms.' It was a lid that was going to be difficult for even the slick propaganda organisation which Britain had built up over fourteen years in Northern Ireland, to put back in place.

2. Other Killings

The acquittal of Constable John Robinson caused a considerable stir among Nationalists. It had not been contested that he had fired the huge number of fatal shots, nor that Grew or Carroll were unarmed. A feeling of anger swept the Nationalist community as he was freed and returned to duty. That feeling of anger was subdued when compared with the wave of fury which was to sweep around the Nationalist ghettoes and ripple through political circles in Dublin when three of Robinson's SSU colleagues were acquitted of another killing eight weeks later.

The three, Sergeant William James Montgomery, 26, Constable David Brannigan, 35, and Constable Nigel Frederick Robinson, 26, had been accused of murdering an IRA man, Eugene Toman, eighteen months earlier, in a shooting incident in which two other IRA men, Seán Burns and Jervais McKerr had also died.

They were freed after a Diplock Court hearing before Lord Justice Gibson. Announcing his verdict, Lord Gibson said he was acquitting them 'without any hestitation or reservation.' He described the three accused as 'absolutely blameless.' He said their action resulted in 'bringing the three deceased men to justice, in this case, the final court of justice.' His remarks pushed the Dublin government into action, but they seemed more concerned about what Lord Justice Gibson had said about three dead IRA men and to the three RUC men he acquitted than they were about the relevations which had been made on other matters in the two murder trials involving SSU men.

The Irish Foreign Minister, Peter Barry, publicly condemned Lord Gibson's remarks and called in the British ambassador in Dublin, Sir Alan Goodison, who was told the comments by the judge were 'entirely unacceptable and unworthy of decent judicial authority.' There was no indication in unattributable briefings given to journalists by Barry's staff that he had raised the matter of cross-border operations alleged to have been carried out.

This was surprising. His opposite number in the Fianna Fáil Party, Foreign Affairs spokesman, Gerry Collins, had been putting pressure on him to ask for an explanation from the British government about the allegations of clandestine operations south of the Northern Ireland border by British forces.

After the trial of Constable John Robinson, Mr Collins had said:

> It was the first time we have had someone saying that he took part in an undercover operation south of the border. The statement was made under oath and was not contested. We must assume it was true. Several important implications follow from this. On the basis of the sworn evidence, the RUC have been operating undercover snatch squads south of the border without the knowledge or consent of the Irish government. This represents an infringement and violation of our territory and our sovereignty which cannot be tolerated. In view of the failure of the state prosecutor to contest the sworn evidence of Constable Robinson, unless some convincing denial is produced by the British government our government must protest in the strongest possible manner and seek a categoric assurance that there will be no recurrence ...
> The Minister for Justice will have to take immediate steps to ensure that if any RUC or British security personnel are found in future on this side of the border they will be apprehended and brought to justice.

He said a very strong protest was normally considered appropriate when events of this kind occurred. It was not simply a matter of people making map reading errors and crossing the border by mistake. 'This time it was different. It was planned and there was a deliberate effort made to cover it up afterwards.'

Mr Barry did not publicly respond to the demands made by Collins that the British should be asked for an explanation. A government spokesman offered no official comment and the matter died in the mass media within twenty-four hours.

The killings of Eugene Toman, 21, Seán Burns, 21, and Jervais McKerr, 31, on 11 November 1982, was the first act in the Stalker drama. All three were members of the IRA. They died on a roadside near their home town of Lurgan after a hail of bullets was fired into the car they had been travelling in. None of them was armed. None had been living away from home — a sign that they did not believe they were wanted for questioning by the RUC. There were no independent eye-witnesses to the killings. Forensic and ballistic evidence presented at the trial of the three RUC Special Support Unit men charged with the murder of Toman showed that 109 bullets had been fired into the vehicle in which they had been travelling.

The RUC men said they fired on the car after it had crashed through a check-point because they believed that they and other police had been fired on. The Director of Public Prosecutions did not accept that story and a charge of murder was brought. All three were acquitted. At their trial they claimed they had been members of an undercover team sent out to capture Toman and Burns whom intelligence believed were on their way to commit a murder. No evidence to support this claim was produced in court, nor was any clue to the identity of the alleged murder victim given.

Evidence from Professor Thomas Marshall, Northern Ireland's Chief State Pathologist showed that Eugene Toman's body had been found lying outside the vehicle, indicating that he had been shot after the car came to a halt. There was no forensic trace of weapons or any incriminating material in the car. An RUC statement immediately after the killings said two of the dead men had been wanted for questioning about serious crimes. There was no explanation in the statement of the RUC failure to detain them at any of the routine check-points through which all three passed each day in Lurgan.

Inevitably, one of the questions posed by Stalker's inquiry team when it came to examine the Toman-McKerr-Burns killings would have been this. The claims by the three accused RUC men that they were acting as part of an undercover mission organised 'by Intelligence' also implied that the sergeant and his two constable companions had been acting with the knowledge of higher authority.

Remarks by Lord Justice Gibson when he acquitted the three RUC men led to a storm of protest. He commended them for their courage and determination in bringing the three deceased men to justice, in this case, 'the final court of justice.' The *Irish Times* responded: 'Peter Barry (the Irish Foreign Minister) was right to protest to the British Ambassador about the extraordinary remarks of Lord Justice Gibson.' The newspaper, in a leader, also called for 'abandoning the shoot-to-kill tactic and disbanding what in Latin America would be called "death squads".'

Thirteen days later, on 24 November 1982, a seventeen-year-old Lurgan youth, Michael Tighe, was shot dead and another teenager was seriously wounded when an SSU squad ambushed what they thought were IRA men who had come to collect weapons hidden in a barn. Two old rifles were later found at the scene. They were vintage models and there was no ammunition with them. An RUC statement said the two youths had been shot after one of them pointed a rifle at the police.

Both were left for dead. Only a miracle of modern medicine saved the second teenager. Neither had any link with a Republican or any other political group. This shooting set the scene for the killings, just seventeen days later, of Seamus Grew and Roddy Carroll twenty miles to the south. The subsequent wave of protests from Nationalist politicians and churchmen was so widespread that it seemed unlikely that similar incidents would happen again.

Two days after Christmas, Andersonstown man Patrick Elliott was shot dead as he ran away from a take-away restaurant near his home, having just robbed the till. He was unarmed. But the killing appeared to be a chance event which happened when uniformed British troops happened on the scene of the robbery and over-reacted.

The following month, on 19 January 1983, another young Nationalist was shot dead on the streets near his home. Francis McColgan, from Turf Lodge, Belfast, was killed by uniformed RUC men when they saw him run off after the robbery of a petrol filling station. A toy gun was found beside his body.

In Derry, an INLA man was shot dead on the street the following month. Neighbours claimed that he had been lured from a house where he was baby-sitting and ambushed by British troops in plain-clothes, who were probably SAS men. The RUC said he had been armed, but later admitted that no weapon had been found.

The arguments about this killing were still going on when the SSU made their next appearance with fatal results — this time on the streets of Belfast. Their victim was a Protestant, William Millar, a member of the UVF, who died in a hail of gunfire outside Queen's University in a stolen car. His death led to speculation that he and a companion had been seen moving guns and that it had been assumed by the RUC that they were IRA men. That killing, on 16 March 1983, seemed to bring to an end a bloody chapter in the history of the RUC.

Fr Denis Faul and Fr Raymond Murray continued their campaign for an investigation into the series of killings throughout 1983. The SSU adopted such a low profile that many believed newspaper reports that it had been disbanded. Its members were reported to have been integrated into the Divisional Mobile Support Units or the Headquarters Mobile Support Unit, the RUC's quick reaction force. But the SSU was still very much alive — and still a force to be reckoned with.

At midnight on 17 February 1984, sixteen SSU men arrived at a block of flats in West Belfast's Corrib Avenue, Lenadoon. With a screech of brakes after the style of a Gestapo raid in wartime Paris, their four undercover 'Q' cars halted outside. The SSU men who jumped from them were wearing an assortment of clothing. Some had dark sweaters, gunbelts and holsters: others wore green rubberised anoraks. None wore uniform headgear. They carried sledge-hammers, shotguns and Magnum revolvers.

They knocked loudly on the door of a flat occupied by Mrs Elizabeth Callaghan. Alone, with her eight-year-old daughter, Martina, she called out to enquire who was there. Her answer came swiftly. The door was broken from its hinges by sledge-hammers and the SSU rushed into the room. Their entrance was an anti-climax. Whoever or whatever they hoped to find was not there.

Undeterred, they tried the flat next door, using the same method of entry at the home of Arthur and Ann McFerran. Again they were disappointed. After a brief glance into all the rooms, the SSU men, shotguns at the ready, left as quickly as they had arrived, roaring off into the wet night in the direction of the Loyalist Suffolk estate.

Precisely a week later, on 26 February, the SSU staged a repeat of the Lenadoon raid — this time in the tiny Nationalist ghetto of Short Strand in East Belfast. Just after dark, six unmarked Ford Cortina cars accompanied by an RUC armoured Land Rover braked to a halt outside the MacAirt Community Centre. A snooker competition was in progress. The SSU men who jumped from the cars were wearing an assortment of civilian clothes. Some carried sledge-hammers or fire-axes, others had more lethal implements — Ingram American-made sub-machineguns and automatic shotguns. Again a door was smashed — because it was not opened quickly enough. Again the SSU men were disappointed.

A month after the Short Strand raid, the two priests who had been following the course of certain events, Fr Faul and Fr Murray, issued a joint statement saying that the public should demand to know more about the activities of the RUC Special Support Unit. They said they found it disturbing that there existed within the RUC a unit with SAS techniques and guns trained in the use of these with 'power, speed and aggression.'

Four days after the priests issued their statement, they had an answer — in the form of a well-informed report in the Unionist morning newspaper, which has long had sources at the highest level in the RUC. The SSU, far from being disbanded, was to have its numbers increased, said the *News Letter*.

On 14 May 1984, the SSU was in action again, with fatal results. Seamus Fitzsimons was shot dead at Ballygally Post Office near Larne. The circumstances of his death and the events leading up to it are as mysterious as those of earlier killings by the special unit. Perhaps because he had no political links, Republican or otherwise, and was an unemployed Belfast Nationalist who may have had it in mind to rob the post office, there was little fuss about the shooting. A toy gun was found at his side.

There is no complete list available of the killings or shooting incidents in which the SSU have been involved since that day, 11 November 1982, when they shot Toman, Burns and McKerr in Lurgan. Some deaths attributed to the SAS or to undercover British troops may have been the work of the RUC's elite SSU. The killing of INLA man Neil McMonagle in Derry's Bogside in February 1983 has been regarded as the work of the SAS, an assumption based largely on the accent of one of the men who fired at him. But a high proportion of SSU men are English, former soldiers who left the army for the high wages of the RUC.

What can be said without contradiction is that the SSU killings follow a certain pattern, one which clearly emerges in the cases outlined above. All the victims were in their teens or early twenties the exception being UVF man William Miller, who was probably mistaken for an IRA man. All, except Miller, were Nationalists. Many had no connection with any political organisation. None of them were 'on the run' or wanted for questioning. All died in the strangest of circumstances.

Killings in Northern Ireland are not unusual. Many of them are brutal and callous, the result of a bitter war which had ebbed and flowed for thirteen years by 1982. Some of those who died have been the victms of tragic accidents, shot by one side or the other in cross-fire or because of mistaken identity. Often, such reasons for death are covered up, to save face, to avoid recrimination.

Arguments about such deaths can be fiercely contested. Was the husband shot by the IRA as an informer a man who was unjustly accused and unfairly killed? Did a teenager hit by army gunfire really look as though he was holding a weapon, or was he shot by a soldier who panicked? Have some of the killings been revenge attacks, provoked by the death of a colleague? Such controversies are inevitable in the atmosphere of killing and counter-killing.

But in the midst of all this, one group of deaths stands out—those which John Stalker set out to investigate. These killings were not the result of accidents, or of a panic reaction by a soldier, or the blind hatred of a drunken policeman. They did not occur in cross-fire, and they did not happen in the heat of battle. They were cold, calculated operations by a large group of highly-trained undercover men from at least two and possibly three branches of the British security forces, the RUC, the British army and M15.

They must therefore have had official sanction from somewhere above operational level. Someone sat down in an office and coolly planned to 'take out' people against whom convictions could not be obtained, but who were an impediment to introducing an element of stability to Northern Ireland. It was this fact that confronted Stalker when he set about his inquiry.

Criminal investigation detectives like John Stalker have a maxim: find the motive and you'll find the criminal. It was a line of inquiry that the Manchester police chief and his CID team were said to follow — with results that were to prove dramatic.

3. Maurice Oldfield

In May 1980, Sir Maurice Oldfield picked up the green handset of his special 'secure' telephone and spoke to his friend and great admirer, Margaret Thatcher, from the top floor accommodation in Belfast's Stormont Castle, where he spent almost all of his time in Ireland. Oldfield was there at Mrs Thatcher's request, coming out of retirement in his beloved village of Over Haddon in Derbyshire the previous autumn to accept the onerous and dangerous job of Ulster Security Co-ordinator. He was the former Chief of Britain's Secret Intelligence Service (M16). From 1970, when he was Deputy Chief of SIS, Oldfield had been closely familiar with the Irish problem, for which SIS had been given intelligence responsibility. He had been a regular visitor to Belfast during the early 1970s and played a leading part in what was to be described by his biographer as 'inter-service rivalry' — the fierce battle in 1976 between M15 and M16 which centred on Irish matters.

His relationship with Mrs Thatcher had been an excellent one since the days when she was involved in backstairs intrigue against the then leader of the Conservative Party, Edward Heath. Oldfield's biographer describes it as a 'mutually worthwhile relationship with Mrs Thatcher.'

The Prime Minister had sent him to Northern Ireland to get to grips with the situation after the death of her old friend, Airey Neave, blown up by the INLA in the car park of the House of Commons, and the killing of the most senior male member of the Royal family, Lord Mountbatten, by the IRA. Now Oldfield was about to break some bad news to her. He was quitting after less than a year.

When he met Thatcher at Downing Street later that week to

explain his decision he had already had confirm
specialist that he had cancer of the bowel. H
with his other troubles — that rumours, possib
enemies, were circulating that he was und
Northern Ireland because he had failed a pos
his private life. Nor did he tell her that he expected his fondness for young men was about to become the subject of a newspaper scandal.

Just before he phoned Mrs Thatcher he had called another old friend, Brigadier Roberts. Finding he was not at home Sir Maurice had spoken to his wife, Mrs Elizabeth Roberts. She described him later as sounding depressed. He told her: 'If they don't get me one way they'll get me another.' As she explained the conversation to biographer Deacon later: 'I assumed by this some kind of smear campaign was being mounted against him.' Was spy chief Oldfield, the man who was to leave such a legacy of intrigue in Ireland, to end his days a victim of the sort of smear campaign he himself had spent a lifetime organising against others?

Fate saved him from the sort of shame and public humiliation which came to Anthony Blunt and other British intelligence figures whose secretive sexual preferences, having made them ideal material for the clandestine world of espionage, led to their downfall.

Although the media in Britain came within an ace of breaking the story, Oldfield's illness intervened. His biographer Richard Deacon wrote: 'The truth is that despite the fact that Oldfield was an obviously sick man, Fleet Street started to investigate the story. A watch was kept on Oldfield's flat in Marsham Street by reporters. All coming and goings were noted. Nothing was published in the United Kingdom, but some editors obviously thought a scandal was in the offing.' Death came between Oldfield's scandal and Fleet Street. He went to his grave with his reputation intact, but only just.

His passing left his work unfinished. He had devised a strategy for sorting out the Irish question which relied on his early experiences in the Middle East and on later lessons from the cut and thrust of Cold War spying. From the latter he got the idea of 'turning' or converting to the British side, key figures in the IRA. It was a scheme which was eventually to become known as the supergrass tem. But it was from his Middle East experience that he took the tactic that was to lead to the Stalker inquiry. It was a plan to 'take out the IRA and INLA 'middle management' — to 'terminate them with extreme prejudice', as murder is euphemistically described by British intelligence.

Oldfield organised a three-pronged attack on the IRA. The first thrust aimed at winning defections of crucial figures in IRA ranks, not necessarily leaders, but those whose presence was vital to its structure in certain areas. In some cases the person identified was not even a member of the IRA, but the provider of an important service, such as a safe house or transport. Having identified pressure points in the IRA the intelligence chief applied the methods which he had used throughout his career to 'turn' professional espionage officers in the KGB and other foreign intelligence services. These were a combination of bribery and ideological persuasion aimed at having a total defection, as distinct from buying the services of a paid informer. The sums on offer were huge. Some people picked up for questioning were offered up to £100,000 and a new identity, new home and job in a country far from Ireland, the sort of bait regularly on offer to defectors in the spy world. (It is doubtful if the promises were ever kept — most 'converted terrorists' got a lot less than they hoped for when all was said and done. Some who were of limited use were dumped in one of the British economic ghost towns of the West Midlands, their only protection being the false name they had on their dole card.)

Some of the 'CT' defectors were left 'in place' — sent back into the IRA not so much to provide intelligence as to act as 'agents of influence' controlling the direction that organisation took.

Oldfield also improved intelligence collection and collation, centralising it and diverting large sums into the new structures. The diverse intelligence agencies were co-ordinated under an ad hoc supervisory group which he named the Ulster Security Liaison Committee. In Oldfield's brief time in Northern Ireland it met at Stormont Castle, from where he controlled things. After his departure, with his successor, as Ulster Security Co-ordinator Sir Frank Brooks Richards, the meeting place moved to RUC headquarters at Brooklyn — to conference rooms near the M15 office. The liaison committee obtained large sums from Whitehall for. the intelligence effort. Elaborate closed circuit television systems which can see by day and night, using invisible infra red floodlights, were installed on vantage points all over Northern Ireland, from Belfast roof-tops to South Armagh mountains. The RUC's already sophisticated computer observation system, based on the older British army 'Vengeful' intelligence computer, was enhanced by the installation of a digital voice and data communications system called MSX, which links every RUC outpost, vehicles and individuals with the central computer.

During the Oldfield period in Belfast, more than £300 million was spent on improving RUC intelligence gathering equipment. But his most enduring legacy may yet prove to be the third prong — the improved system of 'covert operations' — using indiginous personnel, much as he had done in the Middle East as a middle-rank Secret Service man. It was this tactic that brought an SAS-style RUC unit to Armagh in December 1982, leading to the deaths of Grew and Carroll, and ultimately the Stalker inquiry.

Oldfield was long gone before the effects of his presence became felt in Northern Ireland. RUC Chief Constable Sir Kenneth Newman had been replaced by local man Jack Hermon, while the British Army General Officer Commanding in Northern Ireland, Sir Timothy Creasey, was replaced by Lt General Richard Lawson.

Just before Oldfield left Belfast, a Protestant Nationalist politician, John Turnly, the leading figure in the Irish Independence Party, was shot dead in the Glens of Antrim. That killing, in June, 1980, was the first of a series of murders of key Republican figures, including INLA leaders Ronnie Bunting and Noel Lyttle, and the woman reckoned by British intelligence to be the guru of the INLA, university lecturer Miriam Daly. The attacks ended as mysteriously as they had begun, when an attempt to murder Bernadette Devlin McAliskey and her husband failed, and a team of Loyalist hit men walked pat into the arms of waiting British troops outside the McAliskey home, in January 1981.

People who claimed the killings had been the work of a skilled and daring Loyalist gang, (which coincidentally used the sledge-hammer *modus operandi* which was to emerge later in SSU operations) had their view reinforced by the arrest of the Loyalist attackers at McAliskey's Coalisland, Co. Tyrone, home. They were subsequently charged and convicted. There was no suggestion that they had been involved in anything other than that one attack, in the course of which they were fortuitously apprehended.

Those who felt that the whole McAliskey incident, and they included the former MP herself, was too neat, came to the conclusion that a conspiracy had been hatched to draw attention away from the real authors of the Bunting, Daly and Turnly killings. As with many things in Northern Ireland, it was a question of pay your money and take your choice.

The departure of Maurice Oldfield brought new forces into the driving seat of Northern Irish security — Chief Constable Jack Hermon and Sir Anthony Duff — Mrs Thatcher's close associate and her main advisor on security matters.

After the death of her old friend Oldfield, Sir Anthony was moved from his position as Security and Intelligence Co-ordinator in the Cabinet Office and chairman of the Joint Intelligence Committee to take charge of the Security Service (M15). He and Hermon got on well. They first met in 1978, when the RUC man was on secondment to Scotland Yard and where he strengthened links with M15 which had been forged earlier, when he was in charge of RUC training.

The RUC now introduced a novel idea into their Operations Branch. A highly secretive team of RUC men was set up using recruits who were skilled in military arts. Many of them were ex-soldiers who had service with the British army in Northern Ireland. The idea was that they would 'lie-up' under cover around South Armagh, watching for IRA movements from ambush positions. The team of 40 men, wearing unorthodox clothing and carrying non-standard RUC weapons was based in Bessbrook military barracks, a converted linen mill. It was given the tentative title 'Support Unit' but to distinguish it from other back-up units it became known as the Special Support Unit.

It was the personnel from this unusual unit who would later provide the nucleus of the secret group set up within the RUC to carry out special covert operations after reforms of the security structure introduced by Maurice Oldfield. Initially, 50 officers and men were selected for intensive training at the Herefordshire headquarters of the Special Air Service in Bradbury Lines,

Hereford, and at the SAS field training range
Beacons, in the Welsh mountains.

More than half of the new covert operations men
through the sort of gruelling route marches and enduranc to which they were now subjected by SAS instructors — when they had served with the crack infantry regiments like the paratroopers, the Royal Marine Commandoes, or the Royal Greenjackets. At Hereford there was training in rapid and instantly-lethal shooting in the descriptively named 'Killing Room' in Bradbury Lines.

Their three-month SAS training course taught them escape and evasion skills, a necessary attribute for RUC men who intended to carry out covert operations in IRA-dominated areas like South Armagh and West Belfast. They learned how to fire, strip and clean, American-made Ingram sub-machineguns, weapons long favoured by the SAS, and how to use a variety of other non-conventional weapons, including that ultimate tool of the assassin, the pump-action shotgun, its barrel cut short to make it easier to handle and more deadly in close quarter battle.

The RUC secret unit moved to Ballykinlar Army Camp, on the shores of Dundrum Bay in Co. Down for more training. The huts they occupied had been used to hold some of the prisoners rounded up in the initial swoop on 9 August 1971, when internment without trial was introduced. From here, they carried out a number of dummy runs, testing operational techniques and communications equipment which, like their weapons, owed little to RUC standards.

Their 'uniform' had evolved as a combination of whatever was comfortable for each individual. They wore no headgear, but the military-style Bridgedale, heavy, wool sweaters, navy coloured because of the problem of confusion if they were to wear army khaki or RUC bottle green, and the canvas gun-belt and hip holsters which most of them sported, became the norm.

Maurice Oldfield was on his death-bed in King Edward VII Hospital for Officers in Marylebone, when the secret RUC group moved from Ballykinlar to the more salubrious, and secure setting of RUC headquarters in East Belfast. While Mrs Thatcher was making a farewell visit to Maurice Oldfield her favourite spy, secure radio equipment and an assortment of guns which looked more like a murderer's arsenal than personal protection weapons for a group of policemen, were being moved into two green-painted Nissen, corrugated metal huts behind Chief Constable Jack Hermon's office at Brooklyn.

It was 10 March 1981. The next day Sir Maurice Oldfield was dead, but his memory, and his plans for sorting out the Irish situation, were to live on. In a short while, the first of the supergrasses would burst upon the scene, with most serious results for the IRA. The appearance of what was now being called, within the tight circle of those who knew of its existence, the Special Support Unit, would take longer.

The lines of command, like everything else about the SSU, were secret. But five years on they remain the same. Control of the unit is through 'E' Branch (not to be confused with 'E' Division, which is a police area in East Belfast). From the fourth section of 'E' Branch 'tasking' — as instructions for specific missions are called — is given. E4 office is the most secretive section of the RUC — the one which ostensibly carries out liaison with M15, the British Security Service. In reality it has been the operational arm of M15 in Northern Ireland since 1976. Classified organisational structure outlines given to British intelligence officers sent to Northern Ireland show how the inner core of RUC security — the Special Branch or 'E' Department is organised, and where 'E-4A' and the SSU fit into the picture. (See diagram.)

The top secret sections of the RUC — often referred to as 'Echo' because that is the phonetic codeword used for the letter 'E' — are grouped into five offices. These are *Echo One,* which is commanded by a superintendent and which handles administrative matters connected with the Special Branch. It also deals with Special Branch security and counter-intelligence, including the vetting of staff with access to Special Branch or M15 material. In addition it has a number of more mundane tasks. It deals with Special Branch mail and the distribution of internal documents within the Branch and it is responsible for transport, including payment of mileage allowance to officers using their own vehicles and the provision of 'Q' cars — disguised vehicles for use in undercover work.

Echo Two is the legal office of the Special Branch, under the command of a chief superintendent. It deals with the court cases

E DEPARTMENT (SB)

RUC SPECIAL BRANCH-OUTLINE ORGANISATION

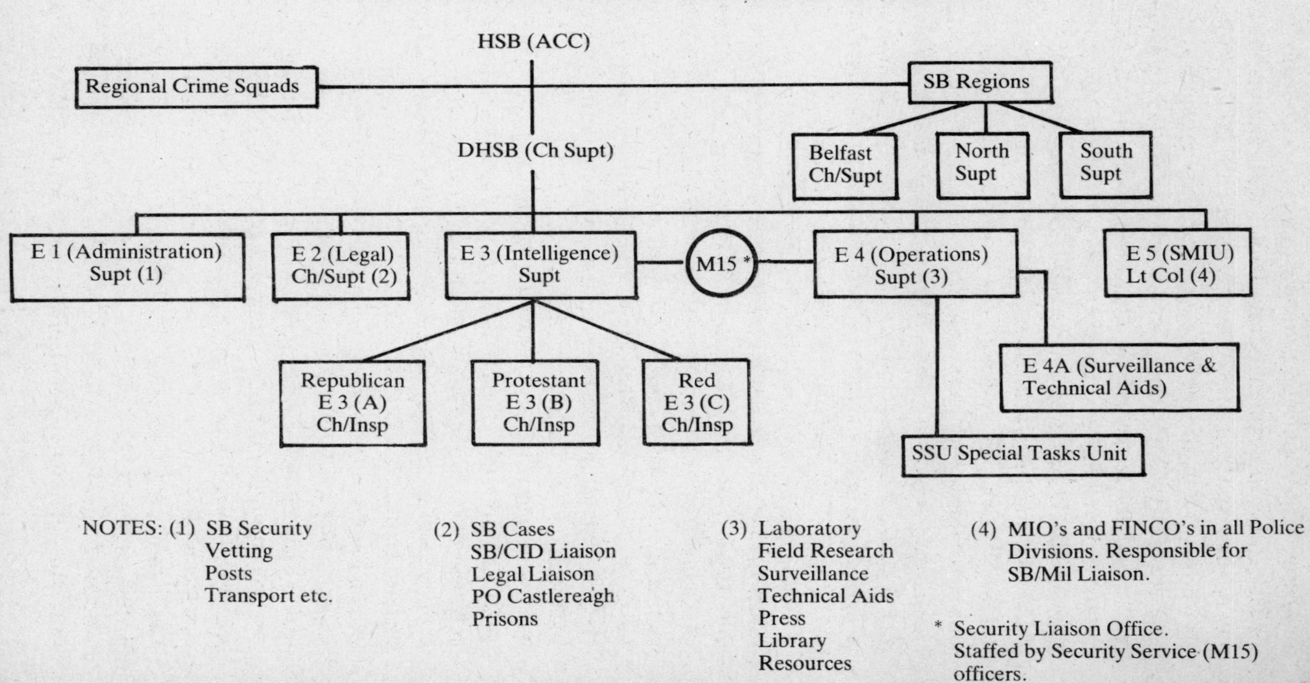

NOTES:

(1) SB Security
Vetting
Posts
Transport etc.

(2) SB Cases
SB/CID Liaison
Legal Liaison
PO Castlereagh
Prisons

(3) Laboratory
Field Research
Surveillance
Technical Aids
Press
Library
Resources

(4) MIO's and FINCO's in all Police Divisions. Responsible for SB/Mil Liaison.

* Security Liaison Office. Staffed by Security Service (M15) officers.

involving the Special Branch, liaison with the Criminal Investigation Department of the RUC, with any matter affecting the Branch and prisons, or the Director of Public Prosecutions Office, and with the Police Office at Castlereagh, a section of Castlereagh RUC Holding Centre in East Belfast. This last duty gives a clue about one of E2's other tasks — liaison with the Registry at M15 headquarters in Mayfair, London, which contains voluminous information on British subjects and millions of other people around the world who might pose a threat to the safety or stability of the United Kingdom, or who would otherwise be of interest to the Security Service. Castlereagh is the place which M15 use as their Northern Irish interrogation centre, unlike Gough Barracks Holding Centre in Armagh, and the now-closed Ballykelly Holding Centre near Derry, which have been used exclusively by the RUC and British Military intelligence for questioning prisoners.

Echo Three is the part of the RUC Special Branch which fits the public image of it. E3 is commanded by a superintendent and is responsible for the collection, assessment and collation of intelligence. It is divided into three parts — E3A, commanded by a chief inspector deals exclusively with Republican groups, largely the IRA and the INLA. E3B gathers intelligence on Protestants (they use that specific term rather than the term 'Loyalists', a reflection of the influence of British intelligence on the RUC Special Branch). E3C collects information on 'Red' organisations (again the title reflects M15 influence). These include the Official IRA, the Communist Party and various Trotskyite groups.

Echo Four is the part of the RUC Special Branch which carries out undercover work. Its routine responsibilities include liaison with the Forensic Laboratory and the Data Reference Centre, the curiously named RUC weapons intelligence unit at Sprucefield, near Lisburn, which compiles information on all guns and explosives found or used in attacks. It also compiles cuttings from published sources and records radio or video material of interest to the Special Branch or M15. Details on journalists are held on its files, along with copies of the 'mosquito' press, political tracts, posters and books.

But it is the other aspects of its activity which brings the Echo Four part of the RUC Special Branch into controversial areas.

Under the heading of 'Field Research' a group of hand-picked officers, trained by psychologists and M15 intelligence men at Ashford Joint Services Intelligence Training Centre in Kent, organised a network of 'turned' paramilitary people. Some of these Charlie Tangos (phonetic slang for CT, the abbreviation for Converted Terrorist) are in Loyalist groups like the Ulster Defence Association and the Ulster Volunteer Force. Others are in Republican organisations like the IRA or the INLA. CTs are controlled by an individual 'handler' who is their only link with the Special Branch — M15 intelligence system.

Echo Four recruits CTs using the usual methods of intelligence organisations to 'turn' prospective inside agents, which include threats, bribery and, surprisingly, most often, persuasion, exploiting jealousy or unhappiness about the treatment meted out by the IRA or other groups. The CT system is quite different from the informer or 'source' system used by Echo Three. Because of its links with M15 it is kept totally from the knowledge of other RUC men, confined to an 'E4 Eyes Only' network in the case of all documentation, while even its existence is disclosed within the RUC Special Branch on a 'need-to-know' basis only.

Echo Four has another task — that of close surveillance. This is a specific method of highly detailed observation of an individual's activity over a specified period. It might last a few days, or occasionally go on for months. Close surveillance of a 'target' in Northern Ireland requires a high degree of skill in covert operations. Most targets such as IRA personnel take elaborate anti-surveillance precautions. A great deal of manpower is needed, with perhaps up to 20 undercover operators being required to give full surveillance cover to a single targeted individual without risking discovery. (For that reason it is not used as widely as most of its prospective targets imagine. Routine surveillance, an organised system of observation of premises at specific times, is the more usual method by which the Special Branch, through E3, collects information). Close surveillance by Echo Four also involves bugging premises used by the target, or unorthodox phone-tapping, carried out through the British military intelligence system which runs an extensive phone interception at distribution poles or roadside phone cabinets. This allows E4 personnel to have instant access to phone-tap information, avoiding the intelligence bureaucracy, and offers greater security for clandestine missions.

The surveillance section of E4 is known within the Special Branch as the Technical Support Unit. Its organisational code designation is E4A. Because of their close association with the Special Support Unit, E4A is often confused with it. When Constable Robinson mentioned the cross-border operation by E4A on the night Grew and Carroll were killed it was assumed he was speaking about his own unit, the SSU. In fact there were at least three separate teams in that mission, the SSU, which did the shooting, E4A, which crossed the border and kept Grew and Carroll under surveillance, and the Special Military Intelligence Unit (controlled by E5) which had an unknown task that night.

E4A personnel almost always operate in civilian clothes, adopting appearances which blend with the environment they are in. Some pose as businessmen, others as workmen or tramps. They regularly carry out their tasks unarmed, because the risk of being identified as an undercover man is greater if a concealed weapon is found. Instead, they rely on their wits and a 'back-up' team of SSU men concealed somewhere near their area of operations.

The SSU, on the other hand, invariably wear uniform, although of an unorthodox sort. Bridgedale, sweaters, hooded anoraks and RUC uniform trousers are their usual dress. But they are seldom seen on the streets, operating covertly in umarked cars, or 'Q' vehicles (disguised transport like large vans). Sometimes they use their own private transport. The Peugeot car used in the killings of Grew and Carroll belonged to a member of 'E' Department.

Ironically, a favoured form of disguise for SSU men is to dress as normal RUC men and patrol in police Land Rovers, while a second team in 'Q' transport travels on a parallel course in the hope of springing a counter-ambush in the event of an IRA attack.

It is this operational trick which makes them of great use to M15 for 'special' arrests and for tasks that M15 would not want uniformed RUC men in divisional police areas to know about. It was probably for this reason that an SSU section took part in the detention of James McGovern, the missing witness in the Dowra case, the incident involving the Irish Justice Minister, Seán Doherty. That affair might have brought down the government of

Charles Haughey, had it not already fallen for other reasons.

The SSU has accompanied E4A teams south of the border on many missions, as back-up 'muscle' — and have been caught red-handed several times in incidents which have not been reported in the media. More than a year after the Grew-Carroll deaths, for example, three SSU men driving a female member of E4A into Monaghan on a surveillance mission were stopped one night in December 1983 by uniformed gardaí, after a slip up in the 'clearance' system which should have ensured no garda patrols were in the area. The SSU men were armed with non-standard hand-guns, like that used by Constable Robinson to kill Grew and Carroll. All four were taken to a garda station but were released after claiming they had crossed into Monaghan to meet a garda contact.

In another slip-up, an SSU team consisting of two four-man sections which went into Castleblaney, Co. Monaghan in August 1982, ran into trouble. Four of them made it back safely across the border, but four others were attacked by a crowd of about sixty people after their 'cover was blown' — possibly because it was noticed by someone that they were armed. All four, were charged at the Special Criminal Court in Dublin with possessing firearms. Three were fined for having firearms without a certificate (£350 each).

An RUC chief superintendent who appeared as a witness for the defence, said the three were stationed in Keady, Co. Armagh, and had gone for a drink in Castleblaney, about eight miles across the border from that town. The chief superintendent was not, as his appearance in Dublin might have implied, the Divisional Commander for the RUC 'H' area of Armagh, in which the accused were alleged to have been stationed, but an officer on special duties at RUC headquarters. No mention was made in court of the significance of the date on which the SSU men were arrested in Castleblaney after civilians had identified them to gardaí. It was 9 August, the anniversary of internment, a date when IRA men gather to mark the anniversary of Internment Day.

Stalker's investigation into Constable Robinson's claim about cross-border clandestine tasks would have led to inquiries into other such incidents, and into the motive for them. The Grew-

Carroll investigation moved Stalker's spotlight onto matters south of the border in the Irish Republic. The link between E4A operations and M15, inevitably brought him closer to the discovery that the British Security Service directed a series of illegal, and in some cases criminal, actions in the territory of what is a sovereign foreign state.

The last but by no means the least important part of the RUC Special Branch is E5 — *Echo Five,* the military intelligence section. Echo Five is commanded by a British army lieutenant colonel, usually from the Intelligence Corps. It consists exclusively of British military intelligence officers and NCOs formed into an organisation called the Special Military Intelligence Unit (NI). Such units have existed in every British colonial war since the Second World War and are formed on an *ad hoc* basis, usually from volunteers from 'all arms' of the British forces (ie. army, navy and air force). For example, there have been SMIU (Kenya) and SMIU (Cyprus), both long since disbanded.

SMIU, which is quite separate from the British Army Intelligence Corps (with which it has been involved in jealous squabbles) has members working undercover in every police division in Northern Ireland, sometimes posing as RUC men. Its ostensible role is to provide a link with local police intelligence, but in fact it is used to give Whitehall, through M15, a system of close, secret supervision of the indiginous security forces. Few scandals break and few schemes are hatched within the RUC which M15, through its SMIU eyes and ears, does not know about.

The involvement of the SMIU in the events which John Stalker was asked to investigate was hinted at when Constable John Robinson took the witness stand. How far Stalker probed into the SMIU and what information he obtained is not known. But any investigation of the SMIU would have brought him back to the role of M15 in the whole 'shoot-to-kill' affair, since the SMIU is effectively one of M15's operational arms in Northern Ireland.

But if the Special Military Intelligence Unit and its links to M15 offered Stalker the key to M15 organisation and policy in Ireland, north and south, and threatened to lead to the uncovering of Maurice Oldfield's 'seek-and-destroy' plan for key Republican figures, it also threatened to bring the Manchester policeman and his team of investigators right into the heart of British intelligence's most closely-guarded secret — *the penetration of the garda síochána which had allowed clandestine missions to take place inside the Irish Republic.*

4. The Badger

The killing of Seamus Grew and Roddy Carroll is the seminal event in the Stalker affair. As a result of that incident Constable John Robinson was charged with murder. He faced not only the loss of his job and his pension, but a sentence of life in jail. Sensing that he might have been merely a small cog in a complex machine, Constable Robinson from the witness-box told some of what he knew about the darker secrets of the cloak-and-dagger work which had brought about his predicament.

His allegations were threefold. Firstly, he claimed he had been advised by senior officers that he should tell lies to cover-up the real nature of the mission that night. To induce him to do this he had been threatened with prosecution under the Official Secrets Act, giving him Hobson's Choice — stay quiet in the face of a murder charge, or risk prosecution for disclosing state secrets. Secondly, he revealed that he had been part of a combined operation by RUC and military undercover personnel which involved at least twenty-four persons. Thirdly, he disclosed that part of that operation had taken place across the Irish border in the territory of the Republic. None of these claims have been denied, either by the RUC or by the British government.

But the story that Robinson told was far from complete. There were no details about how many undercover men had crossed the border and why they had done so. The low key reaction of the Irish government in the immediate aftermath of Robinson's claims and the conspicuous failure of the British government to refute them was puzzling. Dublin did not, as might have been expected, press firmly for a quick explanation, and the disciplining of the person who had authorised the clandestine mission for unknown purposes on their territory.

Was that because the affair was much bigger and more sinister than it seemed? Had there been official Irish connivance with the mission in the south? That is one of the inner secrets of the Stalker affair.

My research for this book in Britain has turned up no fewer than four former British intelligence officers and three former agents who have quite independently given examples of missions undertaken in the Republic of Ireland which have received an official nod of Irish approval. Was the mission of which Constable John Robinson was part one of those discreetly approved operations? Where it was approved — and whether permission came at a political or a security level — is something which the Stalker inquiry might have indicated. The Manchester police chief must have been aware quickly after starting his inquiries that 'clearance' had been given from south of the border for the undercover mission on the night of 12 December 1982.

Such clearance was necessary to ensure that those engaged in the secret mission did not stumble across random Irish security vehicle check-points or routine patrols on the heavily-policed roads around Castleblaney, one of the places visited by the undercover British forces. It seems most likely that the 'all-clear' arrangement was obtained through an agent who had been working for eight years for M15, inside the garda síochána. The agent's codename is 'Badger'. He does not hold senior rank, but has a key position in the gardaí. He still holds that position.

How far the Badger's activities are condoned by higher authority is not known. Evidence has been given to me that at least two senior garda officers know of his links with British intelligence. They met two M16 agents in Dublin through arrangements made by the Badger. Both agents were connected with crimes committed within the Irish Republic, carried out on behalf of British intelligence.

It is against this background that the enormous risk taken by certain senior RUC and M15 officers in covering up the truth about the SSU killings becomes understandable. There was a lot more at risk than the exposure of the seamier aspects of security policy in

Northern Ireland. The whole system of covert cross-border co-operation was threatened if what went on in the Republic in the run-up to the deaths of Grew and Carroll became known.

The connecting strands between the Badger, a garda officer and a man who was to flee from his home in Castleblaney, Co. Monaghan, the day after Constable Robinson made his revelations, were there for Stalker to find. That man, an English-born informer, was a central figure in the Grew-Carroll drama. The two Armagh men had visited his home in Castleblaney, eight miles south of Armagh, across the border, on the night they died. As a result of the trial which led to the Stalker inquiry, he was in a hurry to flee. The informer may have got the first whiff of danger when he heard on local news bulletins that Constable Robinson was talking on the witness stand about an unnamed informer in the Grew-Carroll case. A connection would be made within a matter of hours by the IRA between his house, the dead men and the informer mentioned by the accused RUC man. In all probability he contacted his British intelligence 'handler'. Whatever happened, he got some advice from M15 the next day. A mysterious woman telephoned his home. He hired a taxi, drove across the border into the Co. Armagh town of Keady, walked through the sandbag chicane at the entrance to the RUC station — and disappeared. Three days later he contacted his family to tell them that he had been working for British intelligence and would not be returning home.

The informer had been a member of Sinn Féin and closely associated with the IRA in the Monaghan-South Armagh area for years. He also maintained links with local INLA personnel. He had been recruited by the Badger as an informer in the early 1970s, initially providing intelligence only for the garda síochána. When the Badger was recruited by a Special Military Intelligence Unit man, the informer — like the Badger's other information sources — became a source on which British intelligence could draw. For a number of years he continued to provide A1 grade information for the British by passing it to the Badger. At that time he was a 'false flag' agent — a description used in the espionage business for someone who believes he is working for an agency other than the one which really controls him. In his case he thought he was working for the gardaí, because he was passing information to a garda member — the Badger.

In 1976, a brief but fierce battle was fought between Britain's two civilian intelligence services operating in Northern Ireland, the Secret Intelligence Service (M16) and the Security Service (M15). The SIS which had dominated the intelligence system since 1972, lost out to its rivals in M15. Amid great bitterness and recrimination, the SIS chief, who had been behind the recruitment of the Badger was dispatched to head an SIS station abroad (where he later died). The Badger's handler had been replaced by Capt Fred Holroyd, an officer in the SMIU. Holroyd was another of the casualties of the 1976 British intelligence dispute in Ireland. When he left (plagued by a smear campaign of the type which later affected Stalker) the 'running' of the Badger was re-organised by M15. The informer was allocated a separate handler from the RUC's E Department, now controlled by M15, while the Badger continued to be handled by the Army's Special Military Intelligence Unit.

The Badger not only provided information from shortly after his recruitment at a meeting in the car park of Craigavon Hospital in 1974, he co-operated in organising covert missions by British intelligence south of the border. Capt Holroyd has already revealed in two British television programmes (neither of which produced any public reaction from the Irish government) and in the *New Statesman* magazine, some of the operations which were carried out with the assistance of the Badger. They include two murders, one attempted kidnap and a number of undercover surveillance missions by British intelligence. The Badger's task was to provide details on garda movements which allowed such activity to be carried out with the minimum risk of discovery. Later, he was able to use his position to arrange that certain areas would be clear of gardaí and Irish troops at crucial times, when the British mounted clandestine operations.

Holroyd claims that the Badger cleared the way for the Loyalist murder gang who killed Seán Francis Green, an IRA man living in Monaghan, and who were working to the orders of British intelligence in 1975. Since he has documentary evidence, shown to me, that he was the Badger's handler, his claim, backed as it is by other evidence, is credible.

The links between the Grew-Carroll killing, through Constable Robinson (who was Stalker's starting point) and the informer extend directly to the Badger. From the Badger the connections go in several directions. One strand leads into the garda síochána — to the two other gardaí 'talent spotted' by the Badger in other key areas of the force, according to Capt Holroyd, who were later recruited by British intelligence as espionage agents, and to the senior officers who either condoned or co-operated with a foreign intelligence organisation, M15.

But there were more sinister connections which confronted Stalker. The Badger had been involved as a member of the garda síochána on the periphery of what became known in Dublin as the Kilbarrack bugging, when a hidden microphone and radio transmitter were discovered at a house in which SDLP deputy leader Seamus Mallon was accommodated during the New Ireland Forum in 1984. Another strand linked the SSU with the Dowra affair, an incident in which an innocent man was arrested by the RUC in Fermanagh at a time when he should have been giving evidence for the prosecution in a case against the Irish Justice Minister's brother-in-law who had been charged with assault. The arrest was greeted with knowing nods in the Dublin media, and the suggestion that the Minister, Seán Doherty, might have had some association with the arrest wrecked his career as a minister, and seriously undermined his party leader, Charles Haughey.

Some of the things which lay along the course of Stalker's investigation are, if true, so outrageous that they make the criminal activity in the Watergate affair, or even the accidental killing of a *Rainbow Warrior* crewman by French intelligence officers in the Greenpeace scandal look tame.

For example, one of the operations linked with the Badger was an attempt to murder an alleged IRA bomb-maker whom M15 believed lived near the border. Two attempts were made on his life. The first was organised by M15 through the SMIU, using 'Freds' — agents recruited from Unionist paramilitary ranks who were unaware they were working for M15 and who could be easily denied if they were caught. That mission was aborted for unknown reasons.

A second attempt was organised, using SAS troops who crossed into the 'Monaghan salient' — as the British security forces call the part of the Irish Republic which juts into Northern Ireland. Something went wrong with the operation, and they killed an innocent man. That happened in 1978. The garda file is still not closed on that murder. Stalker's investigations might have added new information to it.

The M15 technique used in the first bid to kill this man is a common one, as Stalker most probably discovered. Another example of it was seen in 1981 when an M15 agent in Co. Monaghan, approached the UDA with the offer of information. He met an UDA commander near the border and provided information on Republicans. Had any of them been shot by Loyalists, few people would have made the connection with M15.

Holroyd's allegations then, made in May 1984, long before the Stalker inquiry are worth examining in detail. They dove-tail with claims made by Constable Robinson and another former intelligence man in Northern Ireland, Capt Colin Wallace, and several others who worked on dirty tricks operations for British intelligence in Ireland, on both sides of the border. Capt Holroyd is bitter about the way he was treated by his former bosses in the intelligence business. Since returning from Africa he has fought to clear his name of the stigma that he was removed from his post because he was mentally unstable. He has won a partial victory. The Ministry of Defence has conceded that he was not unstable when he was replaced.

This has not been enough for Capt Holroyd. In an effort to have those who ruined his career as an intelligence officer appropriately dealt with, he revealed what went on in that part of British intelligence in which he served while he was in Ireland between 1974 and 1976.

The first example of co-operation from the gardaí in the commission of crime in the Irish Republic which Holroyd has disclosed came in March, 1974. A military intelligence sergeant reported to Capt Holroyd that a clandestine cross-border operation was being mounted to kidnap a man living in Monaghan, Eamonn McGurgan. British intelligence had arranged with a garda contact that an area around McGurgan's home in Castleblaney would be 'frozen' ie, left completely unpoliced, while the kidnap took place. The actual bodysnatch was to be carried out by two Loyalists who were to be paid £500 from intelligence funds.

The kidnap plan went wrong when a member of Seanad Éireann, Senator Billy Fox, was shot a short distance from Castleblaney as the kidnap got under way. The kidnappers were stopped at a joint Irish army-garda check-point and the mission was called off. The plan had been to overpower McGurgan, drive him to a border road and hand him over to intelligence men who would wait there with British troops.

Two weeks later, another kidnap operation was mounted — again with assistance from inside the gardaí. The targets on this occasion were Seamus Grew and Patrick McLoughlin, with whom Grew lived in the border town of Monaghan. Three Loyalists were briefed by a British intelligence officer and given maps showing Grew's house, surveillance photographs, some of which had been taken by a member of the garda síochána, and details of his movements. The three men, all from Lisburn, were to be paid £500 for bringing their two kidnap victims to a rendezvous point on the border where they would be collected by intelligence officers.

This second operation went wrong also. Neighbours who saw the would-be kidnappers acting suspiciously near Grew's home called the gardaí and two of them were arrested. The leader of the kidnap gang was a Lisburn man. So sure was he that the operation had been protected from garda interference that he went to a garda station and demanded the release of his companions. He was arrested as well.

He was the link man with British intelligence. In statements after his arrest he referred repeatedly to an Englishman who had briefed him on the operation and provided the maps and photographs which gardaí had seized in the kidnap car. He refused to name the Englishman. He met him regularly by arrangement in a Lisburn hotel and thought he was an army man. There would have been little point in him doing so. The name the 'Englishman' used was false. His real identity is known to me but cannot be revealed for legal reasons. He was an NCO in the Special Military Intelligence Unit, working for the M16 office at Army Headquarters in Lisburn.

The gang were jailed for five years each at the Special Criminal Court in Dublin in June 1974. On appeal, the penalties were increased to seven years each.

More than a series of coincidences connect that case and the Stalker affair. Firstly, the intended victim of the kidnappers, Seamus Grew, was one of the men whose deaths eight years later were to lead to the Manchester police chief's inquiry being initiated after public pressure. Secondly, the member of the garda síochána who cleared the way for the earlier kidnap attempt, the Badger, also gave clearance for the undercover border crossing on the night of Grew's death. Finally, one of the RUC officers being investigated by Stalker in relation to the operation on the night Grew was killed had been named earlier by Capt Holroyd as having links with the attempt to kidnap Grew.

It would thus have been impossible for Stalker to thoroughly investigate the Grew-Carroll killing in isolation, unless he overlooked evidence of criminal activity linked with the attempt to kidnap Grew. And any examination of that case would have elicited details of what had already been revealed by Capt Holroyd — that three men sentenced to seven years in jail at the Dublin Special Criminal Court had been aided by a member of the garda síochána, who supplied photographs, information on persons' movements and other assistance for the purpose of crime organised by British intelligence.

In October, 1974, a 35-year-old Newry man, Eugene McQuaid, died just north of the border when his motorcycle was blown to pieces. He was the victim of a British intelligence killing, according to Holroyd, carried out with assistance from inside the gardaí. The Badger made an approach to an Irish army officer, asking him to assist British intelligence. He claimed that such assistance had been approved by higher authority in both the army and the garda síochána. The officer, however, checked with his superior, who reported the matter to GHQ in Dublin. As a result, an investigation was allegedly carried out which concluded that the Badger was a British agent inside the gardaí. A report was sent to Garda Headquarters to that effect. However, no action seemed to have been taken and the Badger still occupied his key position some time later when Capt Holroyd made his allegations about him. Despite these two independent reports the Badger still holds his vital job. What had happened was that a cache of home-made 'bombard' rockets had been discovered in an IRA hideout south of the border.

The British spy in the gardaí, the Badger, had made an arrangement that arms' caches discovered on the southern side of the border would be preserved where possible to allow an intelligence team from Northern Ireland to inspect them.

Sources other than Holroyd have revealed to me that the team usually consisted of a special undercover ATO (Ammunition Technical Officer) bomb disposal expert, who worked with the SAS and whose code was 'Covert Felix' and RUC Special Branch SOCOs (Scenes of Crime Officers) from E4 Department. The team also examined 'firing points' inside the Republic from where radio bombs or land-mines had been detonated across the border. This arrangement it is said was known and approved by some garda officers. There was also a belief by the British intelligence men who knew about the secret co-operation that the arrangement had political approval in Dublin.

The killing of Eugene McQuaid was carried out as a result of one such cross-border excursion. A British booby-trap expert who went across with a Covert Felix team sawed off the safety pins inside the rockets which had been found in an IRA arms' dump. McQuaid, who was not a member of the IRA, was asked to collect a parcel and deliver it to Newry. He must have known what the package contained. As his motorbike approached a British army check-point on the Dundalk-Newry road he made a U-turn and headed back towards the Irish Republic. The parcel he was carrying on his motorbike exploded almost immediately, killing him instantly.

That night, according to Captain Holroyd, there was a celebration of his death in the Intelligence Office in Portadown, from where the operation had been arranged.

McQuaid and his motorbike might well have blown up on the main street of Dundalk — or in Newry, or some other crowded place, killing scores of innocent women and children. There was no guarantee when the IRA dump was booby-trapped, as a result of the Covert Felix arrangement, that many Irish citizens uninvolved with the IRA or the troubles in the north would not die.

The death of Eugene McQuaid is just another example of a crime which Stalker must have come across during his eighteen-month investigation into the seamier aspects of cross-border operations by British intelligence which were high-lighted by the Grew-Carroll killing. But murder and kidnap were not the only criminal offences committed on both sides of the border, according to Holroyd. Bank robberies, forgeries, burglaries and even a train derailment were arranged, as part of the shadowy war being waged by the intelligence service against the IRA.

Nor were these incidents unique to any specific period in the last sixteen years. Long after Holroyd had gone, new allegations were made in Dublin by another former intelligence officer who had worked in Northern Ireland that dirty tricks were being carried out by British agents south of the border.

What is most remarkable about the Stalker affair is that three former British intelligence men who have served in Ireland and who have knowledge of crimes which they allege were carried out by the service in which they were employed have told me that they offered information about these crimes to the Irish authorities.

Not one of them has been interviewed by the garda síochána. One of them states he wrote to government, shortly after the Stalker inquiry began, offering to make a statement to the Irish security authorities about major infringements of Irish sovereignty and serious crimes committed in the Irish Republic. He says his letter was not answered.

Another offer of information about a quite separate series of crimes, most of them committed in Dublin, was made at a different date by a former British intelligence officer to a politician who was then a senior member of Dr FitzGerald's Fine Gael Party. His offer has never been taken up.

There may well have been many other offers of information made to the Irish government which would provide inside knowledge of dirty tricks operations, or prevent similar activities in the future. Only a short period of research was necessary for me to discover a number of people who have left the sleasy world of intelligence and who because of conscience or other reasons are now prepared to talk about what went on. Stalker's inquiries must have been leading him to just such people.

On the night that Grew and Carroll died members of the undercover E4A Technical Support Unit of the RUC — part of the twenty-four-strong group of which Constable Robinson was a member, crossed into Castleblaney. Their operational logs and official notebooks which Stalker examined seem to have shown they were providing cover for a meeting between an informer and his handler. The Manchester police chief had, at this point, come to the southern link, and found the lid of a can of worms.

5. Destroying Stalker

The 'taking out' of John Stalker was deceptively simple. To terminate him with 'extreme prejudice', as murder is euphemistically called by British intelligence would have been so dramatic an act that suspicion would have inevitably arisen about the nature and results of his investigation into affairs in Ireland. But it was not something that Stalker ruled out. He was well aware, having discovered the M15 link with the activities he was probing, that his life was in danger. Although prevented from speaking freely to the media because of the situation after his departure on enforced leave, his wife, Stella, revealed his fears that he would be killed in a bid to halt the investigation.

Speaking on Granada television, Mrs Stalker said that her husband feared for his life during the course of his inquiry. John Stalker is a level-headed senior police officer of almost thirty years experience. If he told his wife that there was a risk that he might be murdered to keep him quiet, then it must be assumed that he had good reasons for such suspicions, which are all the more credible given his professional training and his background as a CID officer.

The Manchester Deputy Chief Constable was not being alarmist. Murders of convenience are easily arranged in Northern Ireland. A tip-off to a Republican group that John Stalker was a British intelligence man or an army officer who would be off-duty and unguarded at a certain place and at a certain time would probably have been sufficient to 'terminate him with extreme prejudice'. Others like Rev Robert Bradford and John McKeague, both of whom were potentially embarrassing witnesses in the Kincora sex scandal which has been linked with British intelligence, were gunned down, one by the IRA, the other by the INLA, in circumstances which looked suspiciously as though they had been set up by someone with inside knowledge of their movements and bodyguard arrangements. Another leading Unionist, Assembly man Edgar Graham, a lawyer at Queen's University, was also shot dead. A few days earlier he had agreed to prepare a legal case for the European Court of Human Rights which was aimed at exposing the use of Loyalists by British intelligence in the early 1970s.

Stella Stalker, a woman whose life as a housewife in Manchester's stockbroker belt in leafy Warburton, Cheshire, is far removed from the violent intrigue of Northern Ireland, was deeply shocked by the treatment of her husband. She told reporters: 'It's all very sinister. It's unbelievable what has happened. It doesn't add up to me, but perhaps I don't understand the system.'

The RUC understood rather better. In a statement issued from its Belfast headquarters, an official said: 'If such fear existed (of John Stalker being assassinated) and if it arose from the danger to life which police officers in Northern Ireland have experienced over the past 17 years, then that is understandable. If, however, this and other reported statements imply something else then it is deeply offensive to a courageous and dedicated police force and the RUC takes great exception to it and totally rejects it.'

Apart from the undignified self praise, this statement indicated that they knew what Stalker had been talking about when he told his wife that he feared he would be murdered. It also seemed to show an urgent desire on the part of the RUC to dissociate themselves from any allegations that they were behind the dirty tricks department. Significantly, they did not say Mr Stalker's fears were unfounded.

The 'taking out' of Stalker, however, was to be less bloody but no less dramatic than the Manchester police chief expected. The blow fell where and when he least expected it — at his home in Cheshire. A phone call summoned him from leave to the office of his boss, Chief Constable James Anderton. He was told to take enforced leave while allegations that he had been in breach of the Police Disciplinary Code were investigated. John Stalker was effectively finished as an investigator of the covert operations of the SSU, and the scheming of M15 in Ireland.

In March, 1985, a series of poison pen letters began to circulate in

Manchester, making a number of allegations about leading members of the Conservative Party in the city. They accused one Tory Party official, Frank Minta, of being a 'racketeer' and said a colleague of his in Blackley Conservative Association was 'a National Front lover and a fascist magistrate.' The allegations were quite false.

Other poison pen letters named a third Tory figure — businessman Kevin Taylor.They accused him of 'running a phony allergy clinic' of being 'a property speculator' and improperly buying land in Bury New Road for development and of mixing with 'queers and criminals', being a rapist and employing a man engaged in dole frauds. Not a single shred of evidence accompanied these anonymous allegations. Despite extensive police investigation of them for more than a year, it can be safely assumed that, like most poison pen claims, the allegations were a tissue of lies.

The letters had arrived shortly after a row among Tory officials in Blackley, Manchester. One man suspected of being their author was interviewed. No prosecution was brought, possibly because of insufficient evidence. In the normal course of events, such an affair would have been regarded as a storm in a tea-cup.

But one of the men against whom the anonymous allegations had been made was Kevin Taylor, a friend of Deputy Chief Constable John Stalker. And Stalker in the spring of 1985, when the poison pen investigation began, was already creating waves in Northern Ireland, probing well beyond where his brief was expected to end. The Manchester police chief had gone beyond a few shooting incidents, into the darker corners of the intelligence structures to discover who had given orders to the RUC Special Support Unit and how it was linked with M15. With Stalker's investigations becoming more menacing the smear campaign against Taylor became of interest to M15 headquarters in Mayfair's Curzon Street House. As a matter of routine, the police investigation which followed anonymous allegations made against a leading Tory like Taylor to Manchester Constabulary would have been logged in the M15 Regional Office in Manchester. The weapon which the Security Service could use against Stalker was now in their hands.

The turns and twists of the Kevin Taylor investigation are many. For more than a year it was treated as a routine check on unsubstantiated allegations. Then, quite suddenly, there was a dramatic change in pace. But it was not events in Manchester which altered the nature of the inquiry. It was what was going on in Northern Ireland. Stalker, it was said, had delivered an ultimatum: let me get the facts, or I will resign and reveal where and why I was stopped.

The Taylor and Stalker families have been friends for many years. They met through their daughters, who were school friends. Taylor is a self made Manchester millionaire who owns health clubs and develops property. In the 1970s he bought the motor yacht *Diogenes.* In 1981, the Stalkers and the Taylors spent a holiday aboard it based in Miami.

Stalker's voluminous report was being typed up at his temporary office in the RUC service training centre at Garnerville in East Belfast, when Taylor telephoned him from Manchester telling him that he had discovered he was being discreetly investigated by the police. His bank account had been examined by Manchester CID fraud squad officers. Stalker is alleged to have told him that in the circumstances it would be wrong of them to meet until the matter was cleared up.

They met by chance at a Conservative Party Ball in Manchester, to which Stalker had been invited as Deputy Chief Constable, three months later. Kevin Taylor said he believed the investigation into his affairs was really an attempt by someone to get at Stalker. The Manchester police chief did not comment. He was already aware from the lack of reaction to his recommendations that senior RUC officers be prosecuted, made a month earlier, that the matters he was investigating were wider than he had suspected. But the Manchester man was not someone to give up easily.

In May 1986, John Stalker's patience was coming to an end. He had not seen his friend Kevin Taylor for several months because of his now almost obsessional pre-occupation with the web of intrigue which confronted him in Ireland. There were leaks aimed at putting pressure on the Home Office to allow the investigation to go ahead. The Dublin magazinc *The Phoenix* carried a report suggesting that questions be asked about Stalker's report in the Dáil and that the opposition force the government to seek answers through the Anglo-Irish conference security liaison machinery.

A week later, Stalker told his superior, Chief Constable of Greater Manchester James Anderton, that he was going back to Belfast. A report which he had compiled and submitted to Chief Constable Sir John Hermon on 18 September 1985 had been left gathering dust. The 13 bound volumes marked secret were highly detailed, but they only scratched the surface of the affair. The RUC Chief Constable had sent a copy of the report to the Director of Public Prosecutions in Belfast, Sir Barry Shaw. In the lengthy report was a recommendation that a number of RUC officers be charged with various criminal offences. Figures given for the number of RUC men mentioned by name vary. Some reports say only three were named. Others say that another four officers were named.

In the event nothing happened ... at least not to the RUC men Stalker believed had been guilty of criminal offences. None were suspended from duty. Incredibly, Stalker himself got the push. He was called to his Chief Constable's office and told to take indefinite leave.

The massive report which Stalker presented to Hermon is alleged to contain sufficient evidence to bring prosecutions against RUC officers, but the Manchester investigator knew he had not got to the bottom of the matter. M15 involvement remained a mystery. There were many pointers in the direction of the Security Service next door to the HSB (Head of Special Branch) office in Brooklyn, RUC headquarters in Belfast. While Stalker had ended his inquiry into the RUC, his investigations of M15 in Ireland were just beginning. He was determined to find answers. In Belfast he was told that certain information of a secret nature could not be disclosed for security reasons. Stalker demanded the answer and asked for an interview with certain senior officers. His request was refused.

Stalker was not going to take no for an answer. He had been chosen to go to Belfast by the Home Office, and it was there he turned to force the issue. It was naive to believe that the Home Office, closely bound up with M15, would assist. In response he received repeated advice that it was 'inopportune' for him to go back to Belfast. Stalker was not to be stopped. He told his friends that it was up to him to find out the full facts, wherever they lay.

He had few people willing to help. However one willing person was the Northern Ireland DPP, Sir Barry Shaw. He seemed anxious to distance himself from the seamier aspects of intelligence activities. The DPP's office said it would consider prosecutions if Stalker cleared up a few points. That was the lever the Manchester man needed to return to Belfast and press on with his investigation. Armed with a letter from Shaw, dated 4 March 1986, Stalker contacted Sir Phillip Myers at the Home Office and asked that certain officers of the RUC be instructed to co-operate by allowing themselves to be formally interviewed.

Ten days later, the home of his friend Kevin Taylor in Manchester was raided under warrant by CID officers from Stalker's own force. He was not charged or questioned. Instead, detectives took away boxes of documents and pictures, including a snapshot showing Stalker and Taylor at a party together in Taylor's home in 1981. They were looking for material that would prove a link between the two men. In the event, they need not have tried so hard as neither saw any need to hide their friendship. They had met seventeen years earlier at a function in a school which their daughters attended. Stalker, Taylor and their wives had been visiting each other in their homes, having meals together, and had even gone on holiday together.

Two weeks later Stalker announced that he would fly to Belfast no matter what the Home Office thought. He would get to the bottom of things by one means or another. He and two of his detective team arranged to travel to Ireland on 3 June. Unknown to Stalker, his chief, James Anderton, had travelled to Scarborough for a secret meeting about Stalker, his inquiry, and his future. There were four men at the meeting: James Anderton, Sir Phillip Myers and Sir Laurence Byford, the two Home Office men Stalker had turned to for assistance in getting to the bottom of things, and Colin Sampson, the Chief Constable of West Yorkshire — the man who was to replace the probing John Stalker on the Northern Ireland investigation.

The mystery of the Stalker affair had deepened and extended now to England. There was a new, puzzling aspect. Who had ordered the raids on Kevin Taylor's home and office, and why? Who was anxious to find a link between the two men which might be used to discredit Stalker and have him removed from the investigation in Belfast? One thing could be said with certainty. It was not anyone in the RUC. No matter how wide their powers and how great their ability to get things done in Northern Ireland, no one in the RUC had the connections to arrange things like a raid on the home of a wealthy businessman and leading member of the Tory Party in Manchester.

Despite the raids and an extensive investigation involving more Manchester CID officers than Stalker had used to assist him on the complicated RUC inquiry, the only 'evidence' discovered was that 1981 party snap-shot. There was no evidence of any crime committed by Taylor or any of his friends. Nor was there any of criminal wrong-doing or impropriety by Stalker in his friendship with Taylor. Three weeks after the Taylor friendship was given as the reason for Stalker being sent on enforced leave and taken off the Northern Ireland inquiry, Taylor revealed that he had also been friendly with Chief Constable James Anderton, and Taylor produced a photograph of himself and Anderton to prove it.

At that secret meeting in Scarborough, which coincided with a conference of police chiefs, Colin Sampson was told that Stalker was to be removed from his duties as Deputy Chief Constable of Manchester until a disciplinary inquiry was complete. He was also being removed from the Northern Ireland inquiry. Sampson was told he was to take over both the investigation into Stalker's friendship with Taylor, and the RUC inquiry, a most unusual decision. It provoked the MP for the area in which some of the killings had taken place, Seamus Mallon, to claim that there was a major cover-up which 'goes all the way to the top.'

The attitude of the media on both sides of the Irish Sea was summed up by *The Irish Press.* In a leading article 23 June 1986 it said:

> The case of John Stalker grows stranger by the day. Every new piece of evidence adds to the impression that here has been a deliberate attempt to frame the Manchester police chief and to subvert the course of justice in Northern Ireland. There are three elements to this mystery. One concerns the allegations against Mr Stalker. These appear to centre on his associations with 'a criminal' — but the man in question has, in fact, no criminal record and it seems there was not much association in any case. It

is now claimed that the accusations were based on a series of anonymous letters.

The second element, and a more important one from an Irish standpoint, concerns the timing of Mr Stalker's suspension. It came just as he was about to complete his report into the alleged shoot-to-kill operations by the RUC in Armagh and after he had unearthed important evidence from M15 regarding one of these operations.

The third element concerns information given to the Irish Government by the Northern Secretary. Mr King told the Minister for Foreign Affairs, Mr Barry that Mr Stalker's final report was with the DPP in Belfast ... Mr King has since apologised for misleading Mr Barry. Something more than an apology is called for. If Mr King did not knowingly mislead then he must himself have been unaware of the true situation. A full explanation is needed.

The media were as mystified as Stalker about what was happening. But they were not to stay that way for long. The Dublin satirical magazine *The Phoenix* first mentioned connections between Stalker's inquiry and M15 — suggesting that this was the reason for a cover-up.

The BBC current affairs programme *Panorama* took up the M15 theme, but from a different angle. It reported that M15 had been involved in a cover-up, to hide the fact that M15 officers had planted a secret listening device in the barn in Lurgan where seventeen-year-old Michael Tighe had been shot. The story was interpreted by many as being unimportant.

In drawing attention to the Tighe killing, the least controversial, and the only one in which weapons were found, it could mislead journalists snooping into the affair after Stalker's removal. Examination of the Tighe shooting would inevitably lead to some doubt about the motives of his killers. Apart from the word of Tighe's companion, accused of possessing arms and convicted when he recovered from gunshot wounds, there is no evidence to refute RUC claims that the two youths pointed guns at them and were shot down in self defence.

The other effect of the leak about the Tighe killing is that it introduced a hunt for a spurious piece of evidence, a mysterious tape recording which may well yet be produced as an ace to further confuse matters. Additionally, the concentration of media attention on Lurgan, where the Tighe death occurred, diverted it from that vital incident which so interested Stalker — the killing of Grew and Carroll.

6. The Highest Level

One of the crucial things believed to have been discovered by Stalker and his team of Manchester CID investigators was that the setting up of the RUC's SSU and the E4A unit had to be sanctioned 'at the highest level' for it to be given approval for its training programme. No RUC Chief Constable, General Officer Commanding Northern Ireland, or even Secretary-of-State for Northern Ireland had the authority to approve a training programme which included lengthy instruction for a large number of RUC men at the SAS headquarters in Hereford, and at the Joint Services Intelligence School in Ashford, Kent.

That could only have come from Whitehall. One body in Whitehall with authority to approve such a programme was a committee which keeps the Prime Minister, the Foreign Secretary, the Home Secretary and the Secretary of State for Defence fully briefed.

Stalker's insistence on going deeply into the affairs of the RUC's top secret unit had brought him to a position where it seemed that ministerial, and possibly prime ministerial, approval had been given to a covert operations unit carrying out missions inside the Irish Republic. It was at this point that Stalker ran into a wall of silence. His inquiries about where and when training for the SSU had taken place are alleged to have been blocked and he was told that this information was being refused on security grounds under the 'need-to-know' rule. Such details were not relevant to his inquiry, he was informed.

How close Stalker had come to implicating Mrs Thatcher in his inquiry can be seen by examining the control structure for Britain's intelligence agencies. Nominally, the Security Service (M15), which handles counter-espionage matters and has had a heavy involvement in Ireland since 1976, is the responsibility of the Home Secretary. The Secret Intelligence Service (M16) which carries out espionage missions for Britain all over the world, and which also has a substantial interest in Irish affairs, is controlled by the Foreign Secretary, as is its sister service, Signals Intelligence, known variously as GCHQ (Government Communications Headquarters) or CSO (Composite Signals Organisation) — the namc used at its three Irish stations, at Gilnahirk, Island Hill and Comber, in Co. Down. The Defence Intelligence Staff (DIS) which runs all military intelligence, from the Special Military Intelligence Unit (NI) to the Joint Air Reconnaissance Centre, which regularly sends RAF Phantoms on high level photo runs south of the Irish border, is responsible to the Defence Secretary.

But the division of responsibilities is largely theoretical. Mrs Thatcher takes a keen interest in intelligence matters, as did one of her predecessors, Harold Wilson, although for different reasons. Like him, she appointed a special minister to keep her briefed on matters which came up in between meetings of the Joint Intelligence Committee. While Harold Wilson had George Wigg as what Fleet Street called his 'Spy-master General' — a pun on his official job as Paymaster General — Mrs Thatcher appointed Cranley Onslow, nominally a junior minister at the Foreign Office, as her intelligence adviser. But, by tradition, the heads of four services have direct access to the Prime Minister.

The Joint Intelligence Committee runs two departments in Mrs Thatcher's Cabinet Secretariat. These are the Assessments Staff, which provides long-range forecasts about the intentions of parties of interest, such as the IRA or the Irish political parties, and the Current Intelligence Group. This is concerned with up-dating information available on subjects of interest, drawing on both overt and covert sources. Both the Assessments Staff and the Current Intelligence Group are headed by Deputy Secretaries in Mrs Thatcher's Cabinet Office.

The Joint Intelligence Committee, which considers final drafts of reports for submission to the Prime Minister and the Cabinet, consists of the heads of the four intelligence services, the head of the Permanent Under-Secretary's Department at the Foreign Office, who specialises in intelligence matters, the chairman and deputy chairman of the Assessments Staff and the Co-ordinator of Intelligence and Security. During the period which the Stalker inquiry covers this was Sir Anthony Duff — the man who took up the position of Director General of the Security Service (M15) in May, 1985, just as John Stalker got down to probing the mystery killings by the RUC.

Although the JIC has oversight of the assessment and dissemination of all British intelligence (preparing and circulating the weekly 'Red Book' to all Cabinet ministers entitled to be briefed on the latest secret intelligence from all sources) it has no direct authority over the four intelligence services. That is the responsibility of the Official Committee on Intelligence (also known as the Permanent Secretaries Committee) which is made up of the most senior civil servants in the Foreign Office, the MOD, and the Home Office. It is chaired by the Cabinet Secretary. At the time of the events being investigated by Stalker its chairman was Sir Robert Armstrong, Britain's most senior public servant and a key figure in the setting up of the Anglo-Irish agreement which was signed at Hillsborough, Co. Down, in November, 1985.

The Official Committee on Intelligence prepares briefing documents on significant aspects of espionage, counter-espionage and internal security, including Northern Ireland, for its political counterpart, the Ministerial Group on Intelligence. (MGI). This is a steering committee chaired by the Prime Minister, Mrs Margaret Thatcher, which supervises M15, M16, and GCHQ. It fixes budgets and lists intelligence priorities and demands.

Two other secret Whitehall committees are involved in matters which affect the Stalker affair. Both are standing committees which meet regularly, usually weekly, but sometimes more often. They are the 'OD' (Overseas Defence) committee and its servicing group of civil servants, which is known as the 'OD' (O) committee. The chairman of the OD Committee is Mrs Margaret Thatcher. The ex-officio members of the OD Committee are the Foreign Secretary, the Secretary of State for Defence, and the Northern Ireland Secretary-of-State. At the time of the events which led to the Stalker inquiry this was Mr Jim Prior.

The OD (O) committee is chaired by the Cabinet Secretary, Sir

Robert Armstrong, and is made up of the Permanent Secretaries in the Northern Ireland Office, the Ministry of Defence and the Foreign Office. It meets on a weekly basis and provides advice and briefings for the Cabinet members serving on the OD committee.

This complicated bureaucratic structure which deals with intelligence matters and Irish affairs reflects the administrative as well as the political difficulties which beset Whitehall in relation to Ireland. Apart from the Northern Ireland Office and the Foreign Office, involved in the north and south of Ireland respectively, the Ministry of Defence has a substantial interest in Irish matters. The Home Office is also involved.

Because the bureaucratic lines of control are so rigid, John Stalker had an opportunity to follow the decision-making process to its origin. The training of the initial batch of RUC men for the Special Support Unit was carried out by the SAS at Hereford. That had to be paid for out of the RUC budget. The SAS regularly provides training for elite counter-terror groups from British Commonwealth countries. It also trains German, Dutch and French special commando groups. Payment for such training, and accommodation or 'messing' costs for visitors at Hereford is demanded on a 'cost of service' basis, with each meal consumed or bullet used being totted up like a hotel bill.

As well as having to pay on a 'cost of service' basis for training, the RUC also had to pay for non-standard specialist kit, which included American-made Ingram silenced sub-machineguns (not available directly to the RUC because of an American Government ban) and secure, miniature personal radios, supplied through the SAS Regimental Quartermaster at Hereford. Papers relating to the financial aspects of these payments passed through Whitehall. Signatures on them indicate the level at which approval of the arrangement had been given.

One man in a position to know about every aspect of these affairs is Sir Anthony Duff, a close personal friend of Mrs Thatcher and her right-hand man on security and intelligence. During the period being investigated by John Stalker, Duff was the Co-ordinator of Security and Intelligence in the Cabinet Office. As such he either served on or advised all of the secret committees concerned with Northern Ireland.

When Duff was appointed head of M15 in May, 1985, *The Sunday Times* described him as one of Mrs Thatcher's 'most trusted aides at Downing Street,' saying he had risen 'through the Foreign Office to become a confidant of Mrs Thatcher.' The son of an admiral, Sir Anthony is 'a tall man with what is described as an elegant figure, a man rarely seen without his bowler hat and rolled umbrella when he leaves his office in the high security M15 headquarters in Curzon Street House, Mayfair.' The former Foreign Secretary David Owen has described Sir Anthony in *The Sunday Times* as 'a very tough character indeed.'

It was this trail which led inexorably from the RUC's Special Support Unit, through the NI office of M15, which controlled Echo Four section of the RUC Special Branch, to the intelligence bureaucracy in London, that John Stalker was following when he was ordered to take enforced leave. At the end of that trail was the 'very tough character, Sir Anthony Duff' the man described in Fleet Street as 'a confidant of Mrs Thatcher' and her principal adviser on security and intelligence matters.

One of the things Stalker discovered was that one SSU operation was in North Yorkshire, in July, 1982. A mad gunman had gone on the run on the Yorkshire moors having shot a number of people. Barry Prudom, an undercover expert and keep-fit enthusiast, had been given escape and evasion training by the Territorial Volunteer unit of the Special Air Service — the 23rd SAS — before being rejected as unsuitable.

His travels through Yorkshire pursued by armed police, backed up by soldiers and helicopters was the main subject of media attention in Britain for more than a week. The Home Office, the Ministry of Defence and inevitably the Security Service took an interest in the apprehension of the elusive Prudom. At this point the RUC's Special Support Unit was invited to join the hunt.

The *News Letter* in Belfast reported:

'A party of RUC men flew to England to take part in the search for police killer Barry Prudom in North Yorkshire, it was disclosed yesterday. But they arrived too late — the most wanted man in Britain had already been shot dead in a gun battle with police near Malton. RUC Chief Constable Sir John Hermon offered a specialised unit and it is believed it was given permission to bring its own firearms. The specialists were flown in by the RAF from Belfast to the vicinity of the major search. But just before touchdown on Sunday morning Prudom was shot dead. It was the first time that RUC help was sought in an operational role in Britain ...'

The 'special permission to bring their own firearms' could only have been given to the SSU by the Home Office, which oversees all police matters in Britain. It is unlikely that bureaucrats in the Home Office would have advised the Home Secretary to give the go-ahead for the RUC squad, trained in 'firepower, speed and aggression' as they were later described in court, and carrying 'specialised weapons' to operate in Britain without the Security Service (M15) being consulted. Nor could the SSU men have been flown from Belfast to Yorkshire by RAF aircraft without the Ministry of Defence in London being consulted at the highest level about such a unique operation.

The Prudom incident took place more than four months before the first reported fatal shooting involving the SSU — that of the three Lurgan IRA men, Toman, McKerr and Burns — in November, 1982. The Yorkshire operation shows that the existence of the SSU, still completing its operational training at Ballykinlar, was known at the highest levels in Whitehall at that time.

As Stalker started his preliminary investigation by getting two of his Manchester CID officers to take statements from the RUC men in the Special Support Unit who had been charged with murder as a result of the Lurgan and Armagh killings, the RUC moved quickly thus insuring that the buck did not stop at their desks if the matter of cross-border covert operations, became prominent in Stalker's report.

On 9 May 1984, an officer in the RUC contacted the *News Letter,* the Belfast Unionist morning paper, and told a senior journalist in an unattributed interview that the SSU had been trained in Britain. He also said: 'The setting up of the SSU and E4A had to be sanctioned at the highest level. Approval had to be received from the top for the training programme.' The RUC officer also revealed that the SSU had been trained at SAS headquarters in Hereford and that the concept of minimum force was abandoned (by the SSU). He repeated words used by Constable Robinson during his trial that the SSU was trained in 'firepower, speed and aggression'. In the same court, an RUC officer put it another way. He said they were trained to fire at people to 'put them permanently out of action.'

In the *News Letter* article it was also disclosed that 'in addition to the normal weapons used by the RUC, SSU is equipped with the 9mm Smith and Wesson pistol which fires 15 rounds, the Remington pump-action shotgun, and the Ruger rifle. It has access to other firepower, including special sub-machineguns.'

The esoteric remark about the SSU having 'access to other firepower, including special sub-machineguns' — a reference to the silenced American-made Ingram machine-pistols they had been seen with — may have gone over the heads of most Belfast newspaper readers, but its significance was not lost on M15 officers. Clearly, the RUC were preparing the ground to show that since the training and weapons of the SSU could only have been provided with high level approval in Britain, then the operations of the SSU, including shootings which were aimed at putting people 'permanently out of action' were at least approved, if not ordered, by persons at the same level in Britain.

Even before things went wrong with the SSU plan, the RUC, knowing the talent of British politicians for finding scapegoats, had provided some insurance by leaking the news that there had been a major divergence from security policy. *The Irish Times* was told by 'senior RUC sources' that 'a decision of this nature would have to be made by the Northern Ireland Security Committee, which includes the Secretary of State, Mr Prior ...'

The leaking of that crucial clue about SSU training, (and therefore their existence being approved at 'the highest level') also served warning on London that the RUC did not intend to be the fall-guys for M15 or anyone in London.

Stalker may have noted this. And there was another question relating to London. Did Sir Anthony Duff, Mrs Thatcher's confidante, keep secret from her the existence of a new tactic against the IRA? One which had been dreamed up by her departed friend, Sir Maurice Oldfield to 'seek and destroy' key Republican figures, using the SSU? What reason could he have had for hiding it from her? And did her intelligence adviser, Cranley Onslow, who must have known of the decision through his oversight of the intelligence committees, also keep her in the dark? Those are the questions Stalker might have come near answering — if he had been given a chance.

John Stalker was too persistent by far. His fate was sealed by his stubborn insistence in trying to get statements from senior RUC men about the chain of command which directed Special Support Unit operations. He had obtained a statement from one who had made it clear that he always acted in line with instructions from higher authority. Whether these had come from the top level of the RUC or from the M15-run Ulster Security Liaison Committee, set up by Sir Maurice Oldfield in 1979 to co-ordinate counter-terror measures, was not clear.

While Stalker was investigating the circumstances of the Grew-Carroll killings he became aware of the so-called Dowra affair. An innocent man, James McGovern, had been in a scuffle with an off-duty garda in the village of Blacklion just across the border from his Fermanagh home. He had been arrested and taken to Armagh for questioning by the RUC Special Branch at a time when he should have been giving evidence in a hearing alleging assault against Garda Thomas Nangle in court in the Co. Cavan village of Dowra. McGovern's absence led to a dismissal of the case. Garda Nangle was a brother-in-law of the Irish Justice Minister, Seán Doherty. His acquittal caused a fierce political row in Dublin. The cross-border aspect of the Stalker inquiry now had a new dimension which took it beyond excursions by RUC and military special units. It was touching on political and more sinister matters.

The Dowra affair is shrouded in mystery. There are two versions: One says that Seán Doherty used his influence with the gardaí and RUC to have Mr McGovern arrested on the day of the trial so that he could not give evidence, or alternatively sought information to be used against McGovern. Doherty denies this allegation and it has to be pointed out that there is no evidence to show this allegation is true.

A second version is that M15 and the RUC saw their chance of smearing his Party leader, Charles Haughey, through Doherty, and acting on their own initiative arrested McGovern, so that he could not attend the court. Since July 1982 Seán Doherty, and Assistant Commissioner Ainsworth had been carrying out an investigation into the activities of British intelligence in Dublin. Some cabinet ministers, including the Taoiseach, Charles Haughey, believed British agents were engaged in a determined effort to undermine Haughey's leadership. They believed it involved a diplomat in the British embassy in Dublin, agents in several multi-national organisations, and a non-elected political figure, as well as a number of other people including journalists and politicians.

There seems little doubt that James McGovern was discussed at an Ulster Security Liaison Committee meeting in September, 1982. Also on the agenda was the change of policy, the plan to get tough with the IRA. The Special Support Unit was already perfecting its operational techniques. A decision was made to arrest James McGovern on the day he was due in court. The RUC men instructed to do so were members of the SSU.

The use of the SSU was a clever move. In normal RUC procedure, arrests under the Emergency Provisions Act are authorised on an 'SB' form, giving reasons for the detention. Although this is kept strictly secret it is held on file within the bureaucratic structure, for future reference. Stalker's men asked for the SB form issued for the arrest of James McGovern. They were told they could not have it for security reasons.

If Dublin had indeed made moves regarding the arrest it seems they were unaware of the extent of intelligence oversight of the RUC, through the Echo Five (Special Military Intelligence Unit) network, and through M15 officers attached to RUC headquarters.

The use of the SSU in the McGovern arrest pointed to London involvement in the affair. The Special Unit — as the operational arm of M15 in Northern Ireland — were the most discreet parts of the RUC. Normal arrests for interrogation as a consequence of a 'trace' (a piece of intelligence information) are carried out by Echo Three, the RUC's Special Branch intelligence office. E3, however, has regular cross-border contacts. The risk that information might leak back to the gardaí that they had been set up by M15, in a bid to discredit Doherty, and his Party leader, Charles Haughey, was one that could not be ignored. There was no such risk with the M15-controlled SSU.

A missing SB form in the McGovern arrest was one of the things Stalker was believed to be pressing to have cleared up when he found himself as much a victim of the smear machine as Doherty and Haughey had been in 1983 when the story of the McGovern arrest was told, by means of an anonymous letter, to *The Irish Times*.

But Dowra was not the only such affair which Stalker came across. Like Watergate in America and the *Rainbow Warrior* scandal in France which followed the bombing of the Greenpeace ship in New Zealand, the Stalker affair has many curious and interlocking links. They connect various 'covert operations' carried out by M15, an organisation which had a tradition of dirty tricks before the French DST or the American CIA were conceived.

The Dowra affair and the covert operations outlined earlier in this book by Capt Holroyd and other former intelligence men have much in common, not least inter-linking personalities. In another incident — the bugging of a Dublin house used by a key figure in the New Ireland Forum deliberations in 1984 — there is another link to the events being probed by Stalker.

A young electronics engineer, the brother of a Republican activist, was accused of possessing equipment capable of being used for making electronic bomb fuses. He is a nephew of Michael Moyna, the man whose house was bugged. The engineer was acquitted, but not before he had been associated in the public mind with the bugging, thus distracting attention away from evidence which showed the incident had M15 links. The house had been used as a temporary home by the deputy leader of the Social and Democratic Labour Party, Seamus Mallon, during the New Ireland Forum.

After the discovery of the hidden microphone, there was a great deal of public discussion. Two theories were advanced: that the IRA had planted the bug to discover what Mallon was saying about the New Ireland Forum, or that it had been the work of British intelligence or the Irish security forces, for the same reason. The arrest of a relative of the house-owner (even though later acquitted) and the suggestion in court that he had links with the IRA appeared to clinch the case for those who believed the bugging had been an IRA effort. However, there were other factors which might have tipped the balance of public opinion in the matter. One was the bugging of the Dublin hotel bedroom of a member of the New Ireland Forum. A hidden microphone was found behind the headboard. The equipment and the method of placing it were identical to that described by the former British intelligence man who met a leading politician in Dublin City Hall more than two years earlier, when he revealed details of British dirty tricks.

But a remarkable connection between the Mallon bugging and the events which Stalker was investigating was to emerge. One of the key figures in the incident was the M15 agent inside the garda síochána — the man codenamed the Badger. He kept carefully in the background and worked well behind the scenes to create the impression that the IRA was responsible for the bugging.

The exposure of the Badger as a British agent, something which seemed inevitable had Stalker been allowed to push on with his inquiry, would have revealed the M15 connection with the Mallon affair — and provided an example of illegal covert operations directed not only against the IRA, but against leading Irish political personalities.

7. Silent South

Reaction in Dublin to the Stalker affair was almost as mystifying as the case itself. Constable Robinson's claims about RUC activities having been carried out in the Irish Republic excited a limited amount of interest among some politicians when initially made in court, but the response to Stalker's suspension and what seemed to be attempts to sabotage his inquiry was subdued. The emphasis of any remarks made about the Stalker inquiry was directed at the 'shoot-to-kill' allegations made against the RUC and the possibility that the RUC was involved in the cover-up attempt. There was no mention of the claims which had provoked the inquiry — that a clandestine mission had been undertaken inside the Irish Republic in which members of the British army, the RUC, and probably M15, carried out some as yet undisclosed action.

The reaction of the mass media in Dublin to Stalker's dramatic removal from the inquiry was like that of the few politicians who commented on it. *The Irish Times* in a leader on 17 June 1986 said:

> With each passing day the smell from the Stalker affair gets stronger ... As the details of the allegations against Mr Stalker filter through, a case which always looked thin becomes transparent ... It is now certain that Mr Stalker's report recommends that charges of a most serious nature be laid against at least two senior officers of the RUC arising out of the development of the 'shoot-to-kill' policy in and around 1982. It is even suggested that Mr Stalker's inquiries have pointed to complicity at very senior levels within the force.

The Irish Press took a similar line. In a leader on 18 June 1986, it said:

> The RUC has a crucial role in attempting to enforce the decisions of the (Anglo-Irish) Conference and that is why the case of the Manchester police chief, John Stalker, is so important. Mr Stalker was investigating allegations that the RUC adopted a shoot-to-kill policy against several Armagh men. As he was about to complete his report he was accused of a breach of the code of conduct and suspended from duty. New evidence suggests that M15 was involved in one alleged shoot-to-kill operation, and that Mr Stalker's attempts to obtain information on M15 involvement were frustrated at a high level and that when he did obtain his information he was promptly suspended from duty ...
>
> There are two issues here. One is the possible injustice done to Mr Stalker. The evidence of misconduct against him seems very flimsy. It looks more and more as if he has been the victim of a frame-up. The other issue concerns the reliability of the RUC. The force is under great pressure and its problems would be increased by a purge of some of its members. But lack of trust in the police is fundamental to the whole question of Nationalist alienation in the North ... For everyone's sake, the matter must be brought into the open and, if necessary, tough decisions taken.

Clearly, both newspapers, reflecting the view among opinion makers and politicians in Dublin, felt that the Stalker inquiry was limited to the shooting incidents involving the RUC which occurred in Armagh in 1983. Although *The Irish Press* mentions M15 involvement 'in one alleged shoot-to-kill operation' no reference is made to reports carried in that newspaper, and, *The Irish Times* mentions Constable Robinson's courtroom claims, which have never been denied, that he was on a joint operation with British military forces which was carried out on both sides of the Irish border.

Why this attitude, to what is clearly the most embarrassing aspect of the Stalker inquiry, should exist in Dublin is hard to comprehend. It is impossible to imagnine that if a gendarme had made allegations that the French Secret Service had crossed into West Germany and carried out some mysterious and illegal activity there would not have been at least a formal protest and a demand for an immediate and public explanation. Not even brotherly neighbouring states like those in Scandanavia are likely to accept such a situation with equanimity, or close their eyes to a blatant violation of sovereignty. The subdued reaction in Dublin to the Constable Robinson claims faded into disinterest, a disinterest which even the dramatic twists and turns of the Stalker affair, with the clear hint of a high level cover-up in London, failed to dispel.

This followed a pattern set more than ten years earlier, when the first of a series of criminal conspiracies by British intelligence in the Irish Republic was exposed. In October 1972, two English criminals, Kenneth and Keith Littlejohn robbed the Allied Irish Bank in Grafton Street, Dublin, of £67,000. They were accompanied by members of the Official IRA. They had penetrated the organisation as part of a British intelligence plot to use agents provocateur to influence Dublin politicians against growing militant Nationalists in Northern Ireland.

The Littlejohns, having carried out a series of actions which included the dispatch of letter-bombs to people living in the Irish Republic and the petrol-bombing of garda stations, had become so certain their charmed existence as British SIS agents would continue indefinitely that they made clumsy mistakes when robbing the Dublin bank. As a result, the Garda Central Detective Unit contacted Scotland Yard directly, rather than through the normal liaison machinery in Garda Headquarters, and the Littlejohns were arrested in Britain. Both Littlejohns were outraged at their detention. They had been promised immunity from interference by security forces in Dublin. Now that pledge from the M16 controllers had been broken.

In response the brothers revealed what they had been up to in Ireland, and their M16 links, to their London solicitor. They named their SIS intelligence controller as M16 officer Douglas Smythe. He had met them regularly in Belfast, London, Newry and Dublin, having first been introduced to them by Defence Minister Geoffrey Johnston-Smith in London.

A month after the Littlejohns were arrested by London police at the request of the Central Detective Unit in Dublin Castle, 'Douglas Smythe' was arrested by gardaí from the counter-intelligence section of the Detective Branch at the national police headquarters in Dublin's Phoenix park. He was detained in the company of Detective Sergeant Patrick Crinnion, a key figure in the administration of Irish security and intelligence matters. It soon became known that Crinnion, a file clerk, had control of the collation and dissemination of all top grade Irish security intelligence. The man arrested with him at a hand-over of secret files in a Dublin hotel car park was identified as John Wyman, an M16 officer — the man who controlled the Littlejohns and who was known to them as 'Douglas Smythe'.

As the Littlejohn-Wyman saga unfolded, it became known to Irish authorities that a diplomat at the British Embassy in Dublin was also involved in what had been a conspiracy not only to rob Irish state secrets, but to kill Irish citizens (the Littlejohns named Seán MacStiopháin and Seamus Costello, who had IRA links, as their targets). Despite this, the British spies and their garda accomplice walked free.

The embassy official flew out of Dublin without being questioned about his role in the affair. Wyman and Crinnion were set free and followed him to London. The Fianna Fáil government of Jack Lynch, by that action, seemed to give carte blanche to British intelligence to carry on spying in Ireland. The Littlejohns were jailed, for 20 years and 15 years respectively, having been extradited as part of the deal. Both were 'deniable agents' — pawns whose links in normal circumstances with British intelligence would have been emphatically denied had they been caught in Ireland — and as such they were expendable.

In January 1976, new claims by a former agent were made about crimes carried out on behalf of British intelligence in the Irish Republic. A Belfastman who had served as undercover agent while he was a soldier in the Royal Irish Rifles, confessed to having inside information on the bombing of Dublin on 1 December 1972. Two CIE transport employees died and 133 people were injured in a car bomb attack which happened at a crucial time for the passage of an anti-IRA measure, the Offences Against the State Act. Before the bomb exploded there were predictions that concern in the Dáil about civil liberties would defeat the measure. After the bomb horror in central Dublin the Act was rushed through the parliamentary process with little disapproval, when the Fine Gael opposition party changed its attitude to it. This caused speculation that the bombing had been the work of British agents provocateur aiming for just such an effect.

The story the Belfastman told in 1976 confirmed those suspicions. He had been jailed for life in 1973 for a series of sectarian murders in Belfast. His part in these had become known when he was put under close arrest at Warminister Infantry Barracks where he had been accused of assaulting an officer on a training exercise at the SAS field craft range in the Brecon Beacons mountains in Wales.

He escaped from the barracks and walked to Warminister Police Station where he told the desk sergeant he wanted to confess to nineteen murders he had committed in Belfast while serving as a member of a 'pseudo gang' in 1972. The sergeant rang the RUC in Belfast, where he spoke to a superintendent in the CID. He confirmed that the murders had happened as described and said the RUC would wish him to be held until they could send detectives to interview him.

Within a few days, the Belfastman had changed his mind about confessing to the murders. But by then he had made a number of statements. It was too late to stop him being charged. He pleaded guilty to murder and was sentenced to life in jail on 15 October 1973. Because of his guilty plea little evidence was given about the killings and the matter was quickly forgotten as one of the many almost routine murder trials in Northern Ireland.

Two years later, through his family who had been spirited away to Blackpool by military intelligence, he wrote to West Belfast MP Gerry Fitt, claiming that the authorities had reneged on a deal they had made with him before his trial. In return for his silence about the involvement of military intelligence in the pseudo gang he organised in East Belfast which had carried out the sectarian murders of which he had been convicted, he had been promised freedom and a new identity in another part of the world.

He said that Mr Fitt did not respond to his letter. His brother wrote to a Catholic community worker in Belfast, repeating the story and asking for it to be investigated. As a result, the Dublin newspaper *Sunday World,* contacted the family at its hiding place in Blackpool and discovered an amazing tale. He claimed to have been encouraged to pose as a deserter from the Royal Irish Rangers. He was sent into East Belfast with another 'deserter' from the same regiment to organise a group of 'Freds' — local irregulars operating undercover for British intelligence. He supplied detailed names, times and places in the course of his story. He claimed he had been visited by William Van Straubenzee, who was Minister for State for Northern Ireland in Edward Heath's administration in Crumlin Road Prison in Belfast. Van Straubenzee, he said had witnessed the signing of a 'deal' with intelligence officers which would lead to his freedom. The Minister confirmed, in response to a question in the Commons, he had visited a prisoner. He had done this, he said, because the man had threatened suicide.

Details given to the newspaper which could be checked proved accurate. Claims he made about the bombing of Dublin could not be substantiated, at the time. Since then, however, information made available by Capt Fred Holroyd, Capt Colin Wallace and two other former British intelligence officers corroborated what he revealed about the bombing.

Despite the detail given about such a serious crime in the Irish Republic by a man who was now in the custody of the British authorities, no attempt was made by the Irish security forces to follow up his confession. Neither he nor his family, who have significant information about the bombing have ever been interviewed. No attempt has been made to invite them to Dublin to have the claims that he was a pawn of British intelligence at the time of the bombing, examined further.

In February 1981, a former officer in the British Special Military Intelligence Unit (NI) visited Dublin where he sold a story to a newspaper about illegal activities being carried out by British intelligence in the Irish Republic. He supplied names, times and a list of places where various operations had been carried out. He also provided photographs and intelligence papers which were classified 'Secret.' Among the claims he made were that telephones had been tapped, premises bugged with hidden microphones and that burglaries had been committed by agents working for his SMI unit, which in turn reported to the Secret Intelligence Service (M16). The man's credentials as a former intelligence officer were checked by the three newspapermen to whom he told his story. It was found he had been given a gallantry award for his intelligence services in Belfast.

His story, without his identity being revealed, was published in *The Sunday Tribune* newspaper. Despite detailed claims that crimes had been committed by British intelligence in the Irish Republic and that the newspaper had been given information about these, no approach was made to the journalists who had interviewed the ex-officer. Irish security authorities appeared disinterested.

Subsequently, a second former member of the SMIU approached the same newspaper with additional information. He supplied a number of pictures of military installations in Northern Ireland which could only have been taken from the inside and a collection of documents relating to Operation Banner — the codename for military intelligence training for personnel in Ireland. In an attempt to build up the story, journalists working on it arranged to have the ex-intelligence man, a former policeman in England, meet a senior member of the Opposition Fine Gael Party.

The meeting took place in Dublin's City Hall. The politician was given details of break-ins, of a murder attempt, of infiltration of the detective force in Dublin Castle. He promised to bring it to the notice of 'the appropriate political authority.' This was assumed to be his party leader, Dr Garret FitzGerald, then leader of the Oppostion in the Dáil.

The politician later said he had informed the appropriate authority but refused to be more specific. Neither the ex-intelligence officer nor the journalists who checked out his story and found the claims about burglaries were correct, were questioned by gardaí or asked to assist in any investigation.

In 1984 Capt Fred Holroyd, made a series of quite separate allegations about illegal undercover missions by M16 and other intelligence services in the Irish Republic. He claimed on two British television programmes to have inside knowledge about murders and kidnaps, naming two of the victims of intelligence killings which had been carried out in Southern Ireland. Later, Holroyd, offered to assist the Irish authorities in identifying British agents in the garda síochána. He stated that he had contacted the Irish government without response.

Following Holroyd's revelations, which included additional information about the bombing of Dublin, another former intelligence officer emerged from the shadows, Capt Colin Wallace.

Wallace, jailed for ten years for the manslaughter of a man in Sussex, claimed he had objected to some of the things that were happening. As a result he had been smeared by the organisation with which he worked — the British Security Service (M15). Wallace, interviewed by me in Lewes Prison, Sussex, alleged he had been first discredited by M15, then shifted to a less responsible position in England. It was there he had been charged with a crime he did not commit. He claims he was 'fitted up' on the manslaughter charge for which he is still in jail.

Wallace's allegations about illegal activities in the Irish Republic are different from those of Holroyd. While he corroborated much of what the Littlejohns, the Belfastman, the two unnamed ex-intelligence men who talked to *The Sunday Tribune,* and Capt Holroyd have said, he made new claims. These included allegations that Irish official documents like driving licences were forged by British intelligence on a secret printing press in Lisburn. His claims had previously been carried in a series of reports in *The Irish Times,* although Wallace was not named as the source. No attempt to contact Wallace or to seek his help in investigating crime in the Irish Republic has ever been made.

With a track record like that it is hardly surprising that the reaction in Dublin to Constable Robinson's confession about cross-border RUC and military intelligence joint operations should have been muted. The arrest of John Wyman in 1972 seems to have been the only and last attempt to interfere with the activities of British intelligence in the Irish Republic. According to Wallace, who was at the time working with the M16 station in Northern Ireland, the Wyman-Crinnion affair was regarded as a minor hiccup. The Littlejohns were sacrificed, and Det Sergeant Crinnion, who was an important agent, was lost. But the British espionage network remained largely uncompromised.

There are a number of possible explanations for the apparent lack of interest by the security authorities in Dublin in protecting Irish sovereignty in this area. The most obvious one is lack of competence, training and resources. Britain possesses more than 25,000 professional espionage or counter-espionage personnel, excluding its 2,000 Special Branch police officers and its military intelligence forces. Such a vast community has resources of finance and manpower which dwarf those of the Irish Special Branch, effectively the only group in the Irish Republic concerned with counter-intelligence. (The tiny G2 Military Intelligence Section of the Irish army, despite achieving some kudos in counter-spying during the Second World War, is not concerned with civilian espionage in peace-time).

The primary task of the Garda Síochána Special Branch is to guard against internal subversion, the main threat of which comes from the IRA or other Republic groups. External subversion has never been considered a primary area of interest. The small section in C3 Detective Branch at garda national headquarters which deals with external threats to state security and activities by foreign espionage agencies concerns itself largely with Communist and Arab countries. In its prime task of guarding against the IRA, and in its surveillance of likely Arab or Communist agents, C3 relies on British, American and Israeli intelligence, to which it is linked through the 'Kilowatt' intelligence exchange network.

There is therefore a natural alliance with British intelligence among sections of the gardaí. They share common opponents — the IRA first, Communists and Arabs next. This common objective with the SIS (M16) and the Security Service (M15) makes them less likely to investigate dirty tricks operations carried out by British intelligence on their patch. Even when confronted with a series of allegations and confessions by former British intelligence operators who, for various reasons, have decided to reveal what they know, there is still a reluctance to take action or follow up the claims.

This explanation is the only charitable one which can be offered for the lengthy catalogue of inaction in the face of a series of highly credible reports about British covert operations. It might also explain why no request was made for permission to interview Constable Robinson after he had revealed the cross-border aspects of his mission.

There are other possibilities. One is that the security sections of the garda síochána have been so heavily infiltrated during the last 16 years by British intelligence that they are effectively controlled by it. At least four former British intelligence men have made such claims to me quite separately, while the biographer of the late Sir Maurice Oldfield, former head of the SIS and later Ulster Security

Co-ordinator, made clear how well the spy chief had penetrated Dublin.

Biographer Richard Deacon wrote soon after Oldfield's death:

> It would appear that M16 activities in the Republic produced rather better results in this period than they had done previously. Not the least of their tasks was the constant monitoring of the significantly large embassy staff of the USSR in Dublin. Another organisation closely watched by M16 was the Irish-Arab Society. But M16's main success was in establishing agents inside the garda, the Irish army and government departments. One of the most vital informants was a senior Garda officer who (up to 1981 at least) was still in that force. He had not only provided information on the PIRA, but on the activities of the former Irish premier, Mr Haughey, and other prominent political figures.

Deacon, whose real name is Donald McCormick, was not only a friend of Maurice Oldfield, he is a former intelligence officer who writes regularly on the subject and is clearly well informed.

There have been many other signs that British intelligence has infiltrated the Irish security forces. Holroyd's claims that clandestine operations by military intelligence and by Loyalist pseudo gangs were given clearance by a garda detective codenamed 'Badger' have been given additional credibility not only by the events being investigated by Stalker, but by the fact that no known attempt was made to investigate those claims when Holroyd made them.

Political reaction to the Stalker affair in Dublin is less easily explained. Why almost all politicians seem to want to wish the Stalker business to remain on the Northern side of the border is hard to comprehend. Even Charles Haughey, who as Oldfield's biographer and former intelligence officers have indicated was himself on the receiving end of British intelligence operations, steered clear of the issue.

Both he and his Fianna Fáil party have been burned badly on security affairs in the past. The so-called GUBU (Grotesque, Unbelievable, Bizzare and Unprececented) scandal which almost destroyed Haughey politically had a heavy intelligence element. It taught him a healthy respect for the power of British intelligence in Ireland. When he discreetly started inquiries into the bugging of one of the delegates to the New Ireland Forum, Seamus Mallon, using his deputy party leader, Brian Lenihan, as the co-ordinator of the investigation, he ran into trouble again. He had the good sense to pretend he was not involved in the Kilbarrack bugging probe. Thus, it was Lenihan who drew most of the flak from the mass media campaign aimed at convincing the public that the bugging was the work of the IRA, which, as the Stalker affair may prove, it was not.

All in all, the silence in the south on the Stalker affair must surely give rise to public disquiet.

Epilogue

On 24 August 1986, John Stalker returned to his job as Deputy Chief Constable of Manchester. He had been cleared of all charges of misconduct. Stalker told journalists he was happy at the outcome. So were others. The mission which aimed at stopping the Manchester policeman from probing further into certain events in Ireland had been accomplished. Stalker was not to resume his position as head of the investigation team examining the RUC so-called shoot-to-kill incidents and related matters.

His jubilation at having his name cleared was not matched by his reaction to the knowledge that he would not be returning to Northern Ireland to finish the inquiry. Nor would he rule out claims that he had been the victim of a conspiracy to nobble his investigations. He told radio listeners to RTE:

> There are still things to be discovered. There are still things to come out. I'm not going to say one way or the other. I'm certainly not saying that there was a conspiracy, but I think it's a wise man who can say there wasn't.

Stalker said he was confused about the reasons for his removal from the Northern Ireland investigation. 'I'm not entirely convinced by some of the reasons given,' he said.

Not everyone was as confused as Stalker said he had been. Tory MP Cecil Franks called for a judicial inquiry into the stopping of the Stalker investigation and the accusations made against the police chief. He told BBC radio listeners that one of the unresolved questions was whether the cross-border incursions by the RUC and other British security forces were made with the knowledge, tacit or otherwise, of the Irish government. He said:

> If the Irish government did know, what would be the reaction of the Irish public once that came to light and how long would the Irish government survive and indeed how long would the Anglo-Irish agreement survive?

Cecil Franks has been Conservative MP for Barrow-in-Furness since 1983. Unlike other MPs, like the Hull Labour MP Kevin McNamara, he has no special Irish interest. His knowledge of the Stalker affair comes as a result of his legal associations — he is a Manchester solicitor — and his links with the Manchester Police Committee through his friendships in Tory circles in local government in the city, with which he has been involved since the 1950s.

He is an unlikely character to make wild allegations, or to broadcast statements which are clearly untrue. His suggestion, then, that the stopping of Stalker may have been engineered because the investigator had come to the point where he was probing the cross-border aspects of the affair are of considerable significance.

No sooner had he made this suggestion about the real reason for the smear campaign against Stalker than Franks was challenged for evidence. He was unable to produce any, or even to reveal the source of his information. However, even a brief look at Franks' connections indicates that the source for his information about Stalker finding the Irish cross-border aspect came from very close to the senior levels of the investigation.

While Stalker was under suspension, other MPs were beavering away among their security contacts, trying to discover the intelligence links in the affair. Kevin McNamara found that the man who was given political oversight of the Sampson inquiry into Stalker's alleged breaches was the Rt Hon. Roland Moyle.

McNamara, in a private letter to Sir Cecil Clothier, chairman of the Police Complaints Authority, wrote:

> When it was announced that my former colleague, the Rt Hon. Roland Moyle was, as Vice-Chairman of the Police Complaints

Commission, to investigate the allegations of misconduct against Mr Stalker ... I immediately had feelings of apprehension.
You are doubtless aware that when Roland Moyle was a Minister in Northern Ireland he attended security meetings and indeed on occasions, as I understand it, in the absence of the Secretary-of-State, chaired such meetings.

McNamara then asked:

Did you at the time of your appointment of Mr Moyle to look into the allegations against the conduct of Deputy Chief Constable Stalker have brought to your attention, or were you aware of, Mr Moyle's previous connections with security in Northern Ireland? Can you say that at no time the allegations made against Mr Stalker, and at present being investigated by Mr Sampson and supervised by Mr Moyle, originated from Northern Ireland or the RUC or from members of M15 or M16?

Behind the MP's query was the knowledge that of all the people who could have been selected to supervise the investigation into John Stalker's personal affairs, Roland Moyle, the politician who had been identified with British intelligence during his time in Northern Ireland and later, was the man chosen. Clearly, McNamara, as his letter shows, at least suspected M15 or M16 involvement in the smear campaign against Stalker.

He was not alone. Another Labour MP, Tam Dalyell, called for an inquiry into the behaviour of the intelligence services saying they had got 'out of control'. But there were others prepared to dismiss such allegations as little more than wild speculation. This view was summed up by *The Guardian* which said: 'The conspiracy theorists have had a field day, but they have not substantiated their case'.

In the area of secret intelligence, positive proof of skullduggery is virtually impossible to obtain. However, even ignoring the considerable body of circumstantial evidence which points to a plot by British intelligence to destroy the Stalker investigation, and the suspicions not only of a number of MPs who are obviously well-informed on security matters, but of Stalker himself, there is evidence from elsewhere that cross-border dirty tricks were part of the stock-in-trade of the British espionage services in their fight against the IRA.

The Stalker affair, considered in isolation, might be explained away as a series of coincidences and accidents. But to do so information given by former British intelligence men, like Capt Fred Holroyd, Capt Colin Wallace and several others, has to be ignored.

What Holroyd and others have said, including the biographer of Sir Maurice Oldfield, is that the Irish security forces, particularly the garda síochána, have been penetrated to a high level by British intelligence. This is what Stalker discovered, if sources close to him are to be believed.

But the penetration went farther than that, and the dirty tricks operations were not confined to anti-IRA missions. The inescapable conclusion, based not only on the links between the Stalker investigation, the Grew-Carroll killings, and the Dowra incident which had such serious repercussions for politics in the Irish Republic, is that British intelligence interfered with the Irish political system, with a view to making it more amenable to themselves.

There is no clear evidence where such a decision was taken. It may have been made at an operational level, by senior intelligence officers acting on their own initiative. However, given the nature of the control system at Whitehall which oversees the intelligence services and the close interest Mrs Thatcher takes in such agencies, as outlined earlier in this book, the conclusion seems to be that the orders which ultimately sent British agents into Co. Monaghan on the night Grew and Carroll were killed and which brought the arrest of James McGovern in the Dowra case came from the top.

If that was the case, as some British MPs suspect, then the Stalker affair went beyond the investigation of an alleged shoot-to-kill policy by the RUC, beyond the operation of British espionage in Co. Monaghan, beyond the recruitment of some members of the garda síochána as spies for Whitehall to an area where London was prepared to manipulate the Irish political process by causing the destabilisation of an elected government, by means of a smear campaign similar to that orchestrated against John Stalker at a later stage. If this is correct then Stalker had to be stopped at all costs.

It is too early yet to say if the final chapter will ever be written on the Stalker case. The man at the centre of things is now back at his desk in Manchester police headquarters. Two RUC officers who were minor figures in his inquiry have been suspended from duty and may face charges in connection with alleged shooting incidents which Stalker investigated. His successor as head of the investigation team, West Yorkshire Chief Constable Colin Sampson will soon produce a report. It will be of interest to see if it will contain references to cross-border excursions by British intelligence or any of the other embarrassing matters Stalker tried to probe.

Calls at Westminster for a judicial inquiry into the entire affair and into intelligence involvement are likely to be ignored, while in Dublin the matter will soon become just another of the peculiar things thrown up by the northern troubles. Life will go on as before, above and below ground.

The British are great at covering up nasty things that the public should not know about, said Colin Wallace, when I spoke to him in jail.

Will the Stalker investigation, having been mysteriously tripped as it neared the finish line, end the way the Widgery inquiry did — with the RUC being given an acquittal, while the central issues in the matter which Stalker almost exposed are ignored?

The Secret War

An Account of the Sinister Activities along the Border involving Gardaí, RUC, British Army and the SAS

Patsy McArdle

– Why have most politicians chosen to ignore fundamental human rights violations in border areas?
– Are the Dublin governments operating a double moral standard – on the one hand condemning torture in the north and on the other allowing horrific things to happen within the walls of garda stations?
– Are the Irish army supporting the paratroopers and SAS?
– Why are heavily armed SAS men, if arrested, not treated as terrorists in the Dublin courts?
– How have photographs taken by the gardaí during interrogation of alleged suspects ended up in the hands of the security forces in the north?
– Is information being given to the RUC being passed on to the UVF?
– Why is the co-operation so one-sided?
– Is the IRA the cause of the violence or are they only responding to British aggression and loyalist repression of the minority in the north.
– Are the people living along the border disillusioned by political rethoric?

FOOLED AGAIN?
THE ANGLO-IRISH AGREEMENT AND AFTER
Anthony Coughlan

* Is the Hillsborough Agreement a triumph for British diplomacy?

* Have we been out-witted and out-manoeuvred?

* Could the Agreement lead to civil war?

* Why did Garrett FitzGerald say that Northern Nationalists must identify with the institutions of a state whose very existence the Irish Constitution declared politically and morally illegitimate?

* Why did Garrett FitzGerald say that the UDR was not acceptable – but now they must be accepted?

* Is our neutrality now in real danger?

Operation Brogue

John M. Feehan

– *Operation Brogue* examines some recent events in the political life of Charles J. Haughey and questions the role played by the British Secret Service in a campaign of denigration against him believed to have been given the code-name *Operation Brogue*.
– It looks at the reasons why the British would want to destroy Mr Haughey in the context of their military needs to extend their strategic influence throughout the Republic.
– It explores the danger posed to these British strategic interests by Mr Haughey and his unwillingness to allow the Republic to be exploited by outside interests or to be made subservient to them.
– It outlines a number of standard techniques used by the British to mould people of standing and influence to their way of thinking.
– It considers how far the media gave a one-sided account of events to the detriment of Mr Haughey and suggests a lot of pertinent questions which they should have asked but did not.
– Finally it looks at Mr Haughey's role in the future and examines the question as to whether he is the person to lead the country out of its present state of near despair.

The Informers

A Chilling Account of the Supergrasses in Northern Ireland

Andrew Boyd

'. . . the latest in a long line of discredited legal strategies, which included internment and the Castlereagh interrogation centres.'

Association of Socialist Lawyers

'. . . a travesty of both legal and natural justice.'

Martin Flannery, MP

'. . . the courts themselves are on trial.'

The Times, 13 September 1983

'. . . uncorroborated evidence, unsafe evidence, and dangerous evidence was being relied upon.'

Gene Turner from the US Congress

'The practice of giving immunity to the most terrible terrorists and then using their uncorroborated evidence to put someone else in prison is bound to bring the law, those who make the law, and those who enforce the law into total disrepute.'

Councillor Sam Wilson, DUP

'Most of the checks for people to prove their innocence have been done away with. I'm very concerned with the situation.'

Noël Saint-Pierre of the Québec Jurists Association

With one hand extended in what appears to be gestures of reform and conciliation and the other encased in the mailed gauntlet of repression the British have blundered through another fifteen years of political violence. Now they have turned to the use of informers.

Sheltering the Fugitive?

The Extradition of Irish Political Offenders

Michael Farrell

– Should Irish Republicans be extradited for trial by British courts?
– Are the Irish courts and the authorities in the United States in danger of abandoning important legal safeguards for the sake of political expediency?

Sheltering the Fugitive? examines the issues involved in the controversial question of extradition from the Irish Republic and the United States. It traces the history of the extradition of Irish political offenders from Napper Tandy and the United Irishmen to Dominic McGlinchey. It shows that many famous Irish leaders like John Mitchel, Liam Mellows and Eamon de Valera benefited from the tradition of not extraditing political offenders.

Sheltering the Fugitive? describes the background to the recent cases in the Irish courts which led to the extradition of Dominic McGlinchey and Seamus Shannon to Northern Ireland and quotes extensively from the judgements in those and other cases.

Michael Farrell also outlines the history of extradition cases involving Irish fugitives in the United States from the 1850s to the 1980s. He examines the four most recent cases, showing how the US courts have consistently held that offences connected with the current conflict in Northern Ireland are political offences and have refused to hand over Irish political offenders to the British authorities.

He warns that recent decisions in the Irish courts and moves by the Reagan administration in the United States to abolish the clause protecting political offenders from extradition threaten the existence of an important international legal safeguard essential to the survival of freedom movements in many parts of the world.

Northern Ireland: Who is to Blame?

Andrew Boyd

– Why did Westminster remain silent while the Unionists operated a permanent machine of dictatorship under the shadow of the British Constitution?

– Why have the Southern governments let Britain hand over the lives and liberties of the minority to the Orange Institution?

– Is the weakness of Labour in the North due to the fact that neither the NILP nor the ICTU have ever had any policies that would distinguish them from the Unionists?

– What help have Fianna Fáil, Fine Gael and the Labour Party offered to the minority north of the border?

Northern Ireland: Who is to Blame? examines the events and political attitudes and ideologies in both islands that have brought Northern Ireland to its present state of dangerous instability.